Endless Energy:

A Blueprint for Productivity, Focus, and Self-Discipline - for the Perpetually Tired and Lazy

By Peter Hollins,
Author and Researcher at
petehollins.com

Table of Contents

Endless Energy: *A Blueprint for Productivity, Focus, and Self-Discipline - for the Perpetually Tired and Lazy* 3

Table of Contents 5

Chapter 1. Energy Rules Everything 7
    Pyramidal Thinking 16

Chapter 2. Physical Energy Vampires 33
    Sleep, Circadian, and Ultradian Rhythms 41
    Eating for Glucose 53
    Shoring Up Deficiencies 62
    A Note on Water 65

Chapter 3. Emotional and Mental Energy Vampires 71
    The Self-Defeating Mind 74
    Challenging Beliefs 94
    The *Real* Vampires 104
    The Exhausted Mind 115
    Keeping Calm 128

Chapter 4. It's in the Cells 141
    The Cellular Powerhouse 143
    Hot and Cold 155
    The Noble Bean 159

Chapter 5. Energized Productivity 169
    The Physics of Productivity 170
    Eliminate the Paradox of Choice 181
    Motivation (and Energy) Follows Action 191

Summary Guide **199**

Chapter 1. Energy Rules Everything

Money is important. Time is important. But these are not the quantities that will limit you in your life.

Without energy, neither of these factors means very much; nothing really does. Think about it: you could have a huge bank account, but it won't matter one bit if you're confined to your bed with glandular fever and unable to stand up straight, let alone spend and enjoy that money. You could be young, bright and full of promise, but if you're depressed and lethargic 100 percent of the time, all that youth and potential means nothing. Without energy and the capacity for action and execution, all of your best intentions won't matter a lick.

This is a book about the psychological and physiological bases of energy—where it comes from, how we can maintain it, and how to get more of it. You can think of energy as the most primordial, fundamental kind of wealth. Energy—whether it's psychological or physical—is like your personal fund of life itself. It's the well that you draw all your motivation, enthusiasm, and passion from. It's what makes one person's life a boring slog while another person, doing much the same thing, appears to be living with zest and purpose.

It all comes down to energy. There's a great big world out there, and if we're to explore it, we need the physical and emotional strength to get out there and engage with it. Opportunities abound all around us, but if we're too depleted and uninspired to grab them when they do, it doesn't matter how fortunate we are or how many lucky breaks come our way.

It's a little like having the world at your feet, and a map of this world's awesome highways and roads in front of you, but not having any fuel in your car. Without energy, life becomes two-dimensional and gray. You may even feel like life is just whizzing past you, and you're left behind because you can't keep up.

When we have energy, the world is *ours*. We have the spirit and the wherewithal to *grasp* it. We can reach out and engage with others, with our environment, with ourselves, with our dreams. We have what's needed to build our ideal world, one brick at a time, and we have the resilience and spring in our step to appreciate what we already have. Energy is fuel—it powers everything great in life, whether that's creativity, productive work, innovative solutions to life's problems, personal development, rich relationships with others, or simply the joy of having a strong body, a clear mind, and robust emotional health.

The great thing about energy is that in some ways, it can feed on and encourage itself. When you are energized, you act decisively and with conscious intention. You turn down distractions or temptations. You're able to push yourself a little, and grow because of the challenge. And when you grow, you're inspired to keep going, setting up today the conditions that will most benefit you tomorrow. Acting with energy has a cumulative effect, bolstering you against life's trials and difficulties, and making celebrations and triumphs all the more wonderful.

Unfortunately, the opposite is also true. Low energy creates more apathy, more tiredness, more of that listless "blah" feeling that only seems harder and harder to budge the longer it lingers. When you're low on energy, you're more likely to take the easy way out, give up on your dreams because they're too challenging, or put up with negative behavior in yourself and others that you might not have otherwise. The result is a steady stream of self-reinforcing behaviors that create a compromised life that just feels bad, plain and simple.

This is why it's so important to focus on energy. It doesn't matter how many other great things you have going on in your life; if you don't have the energy to engage with them properly, to appreciate them, to bring them to life, it's the same as not having those great things at all.

In a way, we can think of this as "multiplying by zero," a mathematical mental model that preaches the importance of shoring up your weaknesses. In mathematics, it doesn't matter what else is going on in an equation or expression—if you're multiplying by a zero anywhere, the end result is always the same: zero. You might think you're onto the next big mathematics discovery like Pythagoras or Descartes, but if a zero slips in there without your noticing, you're just going to end up with a fail for the day. No amount of finagling or negotiating will impact your result.

And so lack of energy is like the big fat zero that cancels out all your other efforts and intentions, no matter how grand and noble they may be. In fact, you could do your best to keep on increasing the other variables as much as you wanted (for our purposes, well-wishing, hoping, dreaming, good intentions, and self-flagellation), but it wouldn't matter. Even infinity multiplied by zero is still... zero.

A chain, as they say, is only as strong as its weakest link. Even if all the "links" in your life are looking pretty good, they can't do much about that one wobbly link, that "zero" that can break and undermine the strength of the entire chain.

In this book, we're going to first examine ways to make sure your energy quotient is a non-zero, and in fact, is always one of the most powerful variables at your disposal. Soon after, we'll focus on optimizing the rest of the equation, learning to beat procrastination, creating better goals, and manipulating our psychology to be more effective and efficient. Often, you'll find that increased energy is the true cure to what ails you because it allows you to have willpower, dig deep, and reach goals. That's the real secret behind traits like self-discipline and resilience.

Let's consider a real-life example. Since you can remember, you've wanted to write that special novel about cats and murder on the Hawaiian island of Oahu. You have so many big ideas, a real message you want to share with the world, but somehow it never comes together. You wake up in the morning and promise yourself you're going to find time to sit and write today. You can barely sit still because of your anticipation over plotting, character development, and the invention of a new fantastical language (for the cats, obviously). But then after a hard day's work, after your commute home, after housework and just, well, life, you're exhausted. Suddenly, you don't feel quite so inspired. You put off your Great Novel Dream until tomorrow. Tomorrow becomes next week, and then next month. And so it goes.

Let's run through a list of common recommendations for someone in your current position of struggling to write a novel. You could try and take other people's advice on how to write your book. You could read about making better plans and outlines, or join a writing group, or even hire a writing coach to help you out of your "writer's block." These recommendations try to improve or optimize other variables in the equation, but they don't address the real problem. You don't have writer's block, and you don't need a coach. You've just run out of energy, and you're trying to multiply by zero. And again, when your energy's at zero, none of that other stuff matters. So long as that's the case, you're going to keep coming up short when it comes to things that you really care about.

When you zoom out and take a bird's-eye view, you can see so much of what's out there in the personal development realm as merely the hopeless attempt at increasing numbers in the rest of the equation, without doing a thing to increase that big fat zero that will cancel it all out. You could waste unbelievable amounts of time trying to understand the psychological, cognitive, institutional, behavioral or maybe even spiritual dimensions to why you can't achieve the things you've already identified as important. But there's a pretty simple explanation that will help you understand all of this without resorting to all these theories: you're tired. You simply ran out of energy. Your gas meter is out; your battery needs recharging.

After all, at the end of the day we are all *biological* beings; we're all organisms that need energy to work, to move, to communicate, to *live*. If that aspect isn't working well, all the rest of it is utterly irrelevant. So, it's no use talking about motivation or passion or inspiration, or even deeper things like life purpose and vision, if you're exhausted and have already burnt all your life "fuel" for the day.

With this in mind, let's turn our focus from the rest of the equation and learn more about the one element that is quietly undoing all of your effort: that tiny zero that nevertheless has a big impact. We can break down energy—psychological and physiological—into four general categories, and this is well-represented by the concept of the energy pyramid, as put forth by Tony Schwartz.

Pyramidal Thinking

When we put off our work, it's often because we have too little energy to do what needs to be done. When we experience our work as draining, we're too tired to focus, we're easily distracted, and we feel like we can't accomplish the job we've been assigned, what we're really experiencing is a lack of attention to the underlying energy pyramid that powers us all.

This is a bigger problem than we realize, because even more so than time, energy is a finite resource that we must protect on a daily basis. Nothing else you read in this book will make an iota of difference if you don't have the energy to pull it off.

Energy drains, and once it does, recharging is necessary. One great tool to understand energy management is the energy pyramid, an idea conceived by Jim Loehr and Tony Schwartz in *The Power of Full Engagement: Managing Energy, Not Time, Is the Key to High Performance and Personal Renewal.*

The energy pyramid is a four-tiered pyramid with *physical energy* at its base, *emotional energy* above that, *mental energy* in the next layer, and *spiritual energy* at the top. Each of these plays an important role in building up or draining our energy, and each tier depends upon the tiers below to sustain itself. Understanding the interconnected nature of what goes into our energy bank allows us to take charge and create more for ourselves. Put another way, if you don't satisfy these levels of energy and engagement, it's unlikely you will even be in a position to focus, work, or conquer procrastination.

The energy pyramid sets forth a model of energy management that we will follow for the rest of the book, for the most part.

The pyramid points out that we must first notice and improve our levels of ***physical energy***. Physical energy forms the basis for all the other tiers; it's the foundation upon which all our energy needs are built. To manage our physical energy, we must mind our physical health. We must eat healthy, get enough sleep, and exercise.

That may sound draining, and sometimes it is. After all, if you're not used to eating vegetables, indigestion will be the initial response to your newly healthy diet. But with time and persistence, eating well pays off with adjusted gut flora and an excess of energy. Exercise works the same way. At first, exercising feels draining, and we finish our routines exhausted. But after we've done it for a week or two, we start to feel energized when we've finished. What used to be difficult becomes easy, and when it does, it comes with a burst of fresh energy to apply to the rest of our lives.

Sleep, at least, is an activity that always feels good when we're doing it. While plenty of us wish we didn't need to sleep and could keep working without respite, it's a nonnegotiable fact of life that humans need rest. Without sleep, we yawn, have trouble focusing, and eventually fall asleep amidst our required activities. By contrast, when we put effort into getting enough sleep, we're energized, ready for our day, able to focus, and unlikely to fall into an ill-timed slumber.

The best part about the physical foundation of the energy pyramid is that it's not an absolute scale. We don't have to become as athletic as teenagers, as health-conscious as dieticians, or as well-rested as Winnie the Pooh to benefit from healthy changes. All we have to do is find room for improvement, then improve. The benefits are almost immediate, and noticing and focusing on how much better minding our health makes us feel can motivate us to continue.

Once we start improving our physical health, we'll have the energy to consider the next level of the pyramid, *emotional energy*. Tending to our physical needs first is essential because our emotions depend upon our physical health. When we're too tired or hungry or malnourished to think clearly, we simply can't focus on emotional pursuits. Emotional energy is simply being in a healthy state of mind, or at least not being bogged down by negative feelings.

Emotions that don't result directly from our physiological state can help or hinder our ability to work, as well. Positive emotions like joy, anticipation, excitement, or even feeling challenged increase our engagement and our energy. By contrast, negative emotions like anxiety, frustration, sadness, anger, and bitterness crush us like heavy weights.

When we're overcome by these emotions, it's difficult to focus on our work and apply ourselves. But emotions aren't things we consciously choose. Sometimes we're anxious when we know we'll be fine, and sometimes we're angry when we know we have no right to feel mad. Sometimes terrible things happen, and we feel sad or wronged; but even when negative emotions are justified, they don't help us learn, grow, and add value to the world.

The best weapon against these modern monsters is *reframing*. When you face a challenge you don't think you can overcome, don't lament the inevitably of failure, but think about how much you can learn and grow even if you lose—after all, it's exactly those sorts of failures that form the foundation of success. No one accomplishes everything on the first attempt; failure is what teaches us what to do differently in the future. A sense of being wronged and a base desire for revenge against the universe is one of the more common negative emotions that can be easily overcome by a shift in focus. The majority of what's happening to anyone is never bad; it's neutral, and you can make the internal choice as to its role in your life.

Feeling good is essential to doing good. Focusing on those tiny gifts and cultivating gratitude goes a long way toward making us emotionally healthy. To feel good, we have to be willing to let go of negative emotions and be grateful for the positive aspects of all things. Happiness flows freely when we do our part, and when we're happy, we're both more energetic and better at finishing our tasks.

Mental energy is the third tier of the energy pyramid. For us to be mentally energetic, we must first be emotionally and physically energized, otherwise our exhaustion or unhappiness will be too difficult to overcome. Mental energy relates to everything about our conscious thoughts—being able to remain focused and disciplined despite distractions and temptations.

This tier asks us to take control of our thoughts. Instead of passively accepting the first thought that comes to mind, we can assess our thoughts and respond to them in order to consciously choose what we think. Mental energy is about the mental muscles and skills we can exercise in getting things done and achieving goals.

An important part of building mental energy is to enter into tasks with optimism. When we begin with a negative outlook, we presume we will fail. For example, children often won't try new foods because they "don't look" tasty. Often, if we can convince kids to try food despite their initial judgment, they won't like the taste, either. They'd already made up their mind that the food wasn't good, which is the reason they disliked it. But the opposite is also true: when kids look at food and think they might like it or when they're convinced to withhold judgment, they often enjoy new foods.

It's the same with adults and tasks we need to complete. When we go in excited to show what we can do, we often do a superb job; if we go in presuming we'll fail, it's hard to produce any work at all. On top of that, we're drumming up fear from the previous tier while we tell ourselves our efforts aren't going to work.

Aside from optimism, several tools can get boost our mental energy. Self-talk, where we engage in dialogue with ourselves, can dismiss less helpful thoughts and give us truer narratives to believe.

Visualizing the completed project can give a sense of reality to the finished process, and meditation uses our minds to calm the tension we retain physically and emotionally. Even managing our time better can come into play at this level of the energy pyramid, as our minds are what we use to schedule our time and assess how long tasks could and should take.

When we manage our time, guide our emotions, and make sure our thoughts are helping instead of hindering us, we'll have more energy and find it easier to face the tasks before us.

After our minds are managed, we face the peak of the pyramid, ***spiritual energy***. This isn't a religious tier; rather, it encourages us to understand our core values and to align our actions with those values. For example, a person who values helping people might do excellently in healthcare jobs but flounder horribly in sales jobs because their values are met in one career path but not in the other.

The spiritual tier is about finding purpose and passion in what we do, which are the best motivators that exist. They only occur when our actions are aligned with our core values. To capture and increase spiritual energy, we must seek activities that get us closer to our core values and passions, and avoid activities that do the opposite. When we're doing what we feel is important, there is strong motivation to keep going and to feel proud and validated when we accomplish tasks.

Physical, emotional, mental, and spiritual energy are all part of the first principle of energy management. When we attain everything the pyramid implies, we're certain to be bursting with energy, but we won't yet know how to direct and manage that energy effectively. In fact, we may be so enthusiastic about what we're doing that we risk burnout.

How do we avoid that? With the second principle: every time we use energy, we must also allow for its renewal. No one, no matter how much energy they possess, can keep going at full bore forever. Rest is necessary, not just for our physical bodies, but also for our minds and hearts.

When we don't take a break from what we do, we eventually become stressed out and frustrated; these negative emotions are often accompanied by negative thoughts. Both will sap energy quickly.

To prevent this, we must disengage regularly so that our minds can heal. Overuse, even overuse of energy, leads to destruction of the resource that's being overused. Rest is what allows us to heal and grow stronger.

Contrasting with the second principle, the third principle of energy management reminds us that pushing past our limits is necessary for growth. We can't just sit idly, work repetitively and consistently, and expect to improve. We must regularly challenge ourselves if we want to grow.

Dancers know this very well. Everyone shows up to their first class barely able to point their toes. But pushing allows muscles to grow stronger and the body to take new forms. Sometimes it takes years of persistent effort to reach our true goals, but the way to get there is always by setting up a challenge and getting closer and closer as our bodies, emotions, minds, and spirits allow.

Even nonphysical tasks require us to push ourselves into discomfort, as anyone who's done a bit of public speaking will know. Most are terrified the first few times, and often that terror is discernible to the audience. Speakers will shake, stutter, and go over sections of their speech multiple times. At first, it feels like it will never get better, but persistence makes the nervous speaker reattempt their task despite the difficulty. Slowly, giving speeches becomes easier. Eventually, the truly persistent will discover that it's an enjoyable activity. But none of that is possible without feeling spurred on to succeed by the challenge of public speaking. At every level, we benefit from challenging ourselves and pushing ourselves into new and difficult circumstances.

The fourth, and final, principle of energy management states that we must create energy rituals to sustain full engagement. Despite the human ability to think and choose, most of our actions are based on habit. What we do, we usually don't think about. What we have to think about, we usually don't do, at least not for very long! That means it's essential to transform energy-sustaining practices into persistent activities so we don't have to remember or talk ourselves into helpful habits.

This will come as no surprise to anyone who's dieted in their life; generally speaking, any short-term starvation will lead to eating in our habitual way once we shed the weight. What happens next? The weight comes back, and we have to diet again. This pattern is particularly damaging, as each time we fail to make a real and lasting change in our life, the return of the old actions and their consequences feels more and more inevitable. It's not inevitable, but avoiding the trap involves making real, permanent changes. The new way has to be sustainable; in short, it has to become a habit.

Two months of consistently performing any action will generally turn it into a habit, but until we reach that point, we have to put active effort into creating a new routine. We must make a choice not to eat certain foods, to exercise, or to drink a certain amount of water. But commitment and consistency is only needed at first. Eventually, thinking becomes unnecessary; we will have the rituals in place to be healthy, happy, and effective at our work.

Once we have the habits to maximize our productivity, and once we become used to challenging ourselves and resting to recharge our batteries, it becomes easier to direct our energy in any way we need.

When we have enough energy, even the tasks we like to avoid become easy to face.

Takeaways:

- It's not that self-discipline, habitualized behaviors, and intentional and analytical thinking are useless endeavors. No, these are some of the best changes you can make to your life. But you won't be able to learn or implement them, or benefit from them in any way, unless you simply possess enough energy to use them.
- Energy is the battery for all of our thoughts and behaviors. Without it, no other tactics, techniques, or tips will matter. This is essentially a real-life application of the concept of multiplying by zero. If your mathematical equation includes a zero, that means the overall result will be zero. This is another way of saying that energy is often the weakest link in the chain, and it is also the most fragile and elusive. It's important.

- The energy pyramid is a helpful way to think about the role of energy and how to manage it. It has four tiers that depend on each other: physical, emotional, mental, and spiritual. It lays out a blueprint we will follow for the rest of the book. The energy pyramid also dictates that we must rest sufficiently or risk burnout, and at the same time make sure we are challenging ourselves and pushing our limits to increase our energy capacity.

Chapter 2. Physical Energy Vampires

In a world where so much is abstract and verbal, it's easy to forget we don't actually live "in our heads" and at the end of the day, our quality of life is directly related to how healthy we are *physically*. An energy "vampire" is what it sounds like: something that sucks us dry of our life force, physically, and leaves us tired and weak. Just like the energy pyramid mentioned in the previous chapter, this is the baseline of what's needed to set yourself up for success.

We're all imbued with *some* energy on a daily basis, but even the most vigorous person doesn't have an infinite supply. To make it worse, there are aspects of everyday life that will gladly sap energy from us if we're not careful, leaving us unable to spend that energy on the things we truly value.

Energy vampires are like leeches or parasites—and sometimes we can be living with them for so long we don't even realize they're there, quietly draining us of our life and enthusiasm. We might not even realize we're in a passive, negative state because of these vampires, but we nevertheless are trapped in that vicious cycle. You might be aware of many of these vampires in your own life right now, and might be making active efforts to moderate their influence on you. But there are still other, imperceptible forces that could act like invisible, underground leaks in your psyche.

Imagine a woman who's been working in a job she actively hates for years. Picture how she has to force herself, day in and day out, to sit at her desk, to answer calls, to go to meetings—all the while despising the work but feeling powerless to do much about it. At the same time she's in a relationship that just isn't working for her—this partner is inattentive, doesn't pull their weight, and leaves the woman feeling like she spends all her mental energy justifying to herself just exactly why she hasn't mustered up the guts to leave.

It might sound silly, but such a woman could, after months and months, sit down on her sofa one evening and feel an overwhelming urge to cry. She could wonder if she's depressed, or worse, conclude that life is always this unpleasant and hopeless. But all that's happened is she's lost awareness of just how thoroughly depleted she is, energy-wise. If she hasn't slept well for weeks, is eating junk food more often than not and just came down with a slight cold, this feeling is going to be even worse. It's no use formulating this crisis as a relationship or career problem—although it may well be. In the bigger picture, before anything useful can happen, the woman needs to bring her big fat energy zero into the positive again.

We talked about the energy pyramid earlier on, and determined the four main elements of energy. In this chapter, let's focus on the purely physical aspect, since in many ways this is the most fundamental. Having your energy at zero (i.e., being fatigued) is the worst you can feel while still appearing relatively normal to others. Fatigue is not simply being sleepy because you had a poor rest the night before. Neither is it the feeling you get from being sore or tired after a hard workout at the gym. Importantly, fatigue can be felt in slightly different ways for different people.

Some may feel extra heavy, as though they were walking around with a 300-pound bodysuit on. Others might feel slowed down or like they're in a fog and everything is getting blurry and washed out. Deep fatigue is like an extra-bad hangover, or feeling jet-lagged after a round-the-world flight. It can also feel like those tender, painful sensations you get all over your body as a flu is coming over you—your entire system just feels weaker, slower, and more overwhelmed.

When you're fatigued and your energy is low, everything feels harder than it normally does. You no longer have the patience, the acuity, the enthusiasm or the tolerance to deal with basically anything that comes your way. If you've been fatigued for a very long time, you may find yourself feeling as though you're crawling through molasses, unable to complete even the most basic of physical tasks without extreme effort. Many people limp along in this condition for truly alarming periods of time, propped up by caffeine and medication to get them through the days long after their bodies have more or less given up. The end result is that your life is being interfered with, and you are physically unable to do what you want or intend.

Physical energy vampires are obvious, and pretty common-sense to identify. If you're starving and so sleepy you're nodding off at noon, it's clear you need to take better care of your diet and sleep schedule. With most physical energy vampires, the problem is not a lack of awareness, but merely a question of improving and changing habits. For most of us, it's easy enough to know that we are tired and run-down.

To get rid of physical energy vampires, we need to make sure we're setting up healthy habits—a concept that's *simple*, but perhaps not so *easy* to put into practice. Pushing too hard and not listening to your body's limits can lead to your body politely (or not so politely!) reminding you to take a break. We all live busy lives, and many of us carry on as though our energy, resources, and time are infinite. But if your natural limits are not respected, sooner or later you will have to pay. Fatigue and tiredness that are ignored for long enough could eventually lead to full-blown burnout, i.e. the gas tank is completely empty and even the reserve fuel is burnt up and gone. The body is, in the end, in charge. When it's had enough, it's had enough, and at some point it will do what it needs to for self-protection.

It's important to recognize the early signs of serious fatigue before it turns into burnout. What starts out as a physical phenomenon can in time bleed over into every area of life, making us emotionally, cognitively, and socially exhausted, too. Whether you're a high achiever or simply pushed too far by external circumstances, look out for the following signs of burnout:

First of all, be aware that burnout doesn't happen all at once, but insidiously, creeping up on you. Chronic stress and lack of self-care can ratchet up until you're no longer able to function normally. But your body will give plenty of warning signs before this happens. You may feel tired for most of the day, most days. You may even dread the thought of having to do things while feeling so drained. You could suffer from insomnia or disturbed sleep, and have difficulty concentrating, or else feel quite forgetful.

Physically, you may feel dizzy or get headaches, feel short of breath or even experience chest pains, palpitations, and stomach trouble. In general, your body feels weaker somehow, and you may be more prone to illness and infection. Your appetite may vanish. Some people may experience a dull sense of being on edge all the time, or worrying endlessly. Physical symptoms seem to translate emotionally into feelings of hopelessness, guilt, worthlessness or just sadness. This depression could also manifest as anger or being irritated with others, snapping at others or losing your temper.

You may not really notice it at first, but you stop deriving joy from things that used to make you happy. Find yourself feeling avoidant and pessimistic? It could be the early warning signs of burnout. You may notice your inner "self-talk" get quite negative and judgmental, perhaps leading you to want to withdraw from friends and family, not quite having the energy to bother with socializing.

Eventually, you may start feeling quite detached from the world as a whole, almost like a zombie disconnected from others and from life itself. You might want to physically remove yourself from work or family obligations, avoiding all interactions with others. Apathy, irritability, and the massive, lurching feeling of "what's the point?" are all signs of burnout.

Now, simply saying "rest" as the solution to fatigue and exhaustion sounds pretty obvious. Yet, many people are unaware of how they're actively failing to maintain their own self-care, and undermining their physical energy and well-being every day. The fact remains that the single biggest energy vampire is disturbed, poor-quality sleep—or simply not enough sleep of any kind.

This seems like an easy solution until you realize that great sleep hygiene is actually a skill to develop and a habit that needs constant, conscious attention to maintain. It's like a gym schedule or a healthy diet: it doesn't just happen on its own!

Sleep, Circadian, and Ultradian Rhythms

How do we improve our sleep?

The first step is to understand your sleep biology, and the next is to learn to work with it so you're waking up refreshed each morning and with a full "tank." Your circadian rhythm is your body's own inbuilt sense of when to wake and when to sleep. Parts of your body perceive and respond to changes in light around you and move through cycles, with physical and behavioral changes occurring over a twenty-four-hour period.

Interfere with this cycle and you push against your body's own physiological "clock." A common way we all do this is to surround ourselves with harsh, artificial light at times of the day that our ancestors would have spent in darkness or low light. Your rhythms are set by light in the environment. If you're in the habit of using LED displays on devices a few hours before bed, starting to phase them out can do wonders for your sleep quality. If you must use these devices, install apps that turn down the blue light and amp up the yellow, or else dial down the screen brightness completely.

Just as fading light signals bedtime to your body, bright light indicates that it's time to wake up. When you wake up in the morning, make a habit of exposing yourself to bright sunlight as soon as possible after you wake, to kick-start your system. In fact, when it comes to sleep, routine and consistency are the goal. Pay attention to the times you wake up and go to sleep, and maintain a fixed routine, making sure to keep your sleeping hours properly dark and your waking hours as bright as possible. Do everything you can to cut down on blinking lights in your bedroom, and invest in blackout curtains, especially in summer. Keep naps to a minimum (twenty minutes at most) and time them for early afternoon, no later.

Finally, take some time to figure out your "chronotype"—i.e., your unique pattern of wakefulness. Are you an early riser who goes to bed early too? Or are you a night owl who only really peps up at around 10:30 in the morning? We're all different, and this has been borne out through psychological testing and categorizing of people into larks (early birds) or night owls. The key is to recognize and respect your own needs and limitations. If you've always been someone who falls asleep early in the evening, go with it. Wake early, do most of your work and exercise in the morning, and allow yourself to cycle down naturally as the day wears on. Make adjustments so that you work with rather than against your natural rhythms.

Mental and emotional factors play heavily into the quality of sleep, too. We know that a poor night's sleep will leave you feeling bad during the day, but the experiences you have in your waking life can carry over to your sleep, too. In fact, many people's sleep disorders are vicious cycles, and reinforcing behaviors that keep poor sleep habits going.

Do whatever you can to reduce stress in your life. Take frequent breaks throughout the day. Even a five-minute pause to meditate quietly or focus on deep breathing is enough to lower your cortisol levels and help you find your center again. One of the best things you can do to improve your sleep quality is to have a daily bedtime ritual you can depend on. You can decide on exactly what will work for you, but the important thing is that it's a habit, and it's something that signals your body that it's time for sleep.

Do stressful, energetic things earlier on in the day and save quieter, slower activities for before bed. Avoid excess stimulation (like exercise, stressful work, emotional arguments or upsetting TV) in the evening and do things that calm you down. A hot bath, visualization, massage, yoga, a little light reading, or taking the time to do a little beauty ritual will all put you in a relaxed state of mind.

If you're someone who has difficulty with insomnia or poor sleep hygiene, a big part of your ritual will be to program yourself with a more relaxed attitude toward sleep in general. Deliberately take the time to wind down and empty your thoughts. Tell yourself it's not the end of the world if you don't sleep properly; just relax, take your time, and rest. If you haven't fallen asleep after around twenty minutes, get up out of bed and go somewhere else to do a calming activity. A cup of tea, a doodle in a journal or listening to a quiet podcast are all great ideas.

Insomnia can feed on itself if you allow yourself to *worry* that you're not sleeping well. Your attitude toward sleep is just as important as the more practical factors. Actively remind yourself, "It's OK if I don't fall asleep. I'll still get rest even if I just hang out here for a while." Don't put pressure on yourself to "sleep right." What could be more un-relaxing than that?

If you can't fall asleep, don't linger in bed, or else you may create negative associations with that space. It's a good idea to reserve this area for sleep and sex solely. You might find that spending a little time making your own "sleep sanctuary" goes a long way toward telling your unconscious mind what to expect when you get into bed. Choose relaxing, decluttered décor. Good-quality bedding, blackout curtains, breathable pajamas, and possibly sleep masks and earplugs will do wonders. Ensure your mattress is firm and doesn't keep you overly hot, and that the room is quiet, dark, and slightly colder than you'd normally like. Make sure there's good air flow without any drafts. Do something about snoring partners and/or pets who hog all the space! Get yourself a pillow you love and you're ready to go.

Finally, if you're a frequent flyer or find yourself sleeping in hotels often, take some time to figure out ways to mediate the disruption. Over-the-counter melatonin pills can help with jet lag, and the occasional sleeping pill or natural remedy can help break a bad sleep cycle—when used only very occasionally, that is.

Overall, there's a lot you can do to honor your natural limits and needs, and work with your biology rather than fight it (in case you haven't noticed, the latter never works out well anyway.) And this goes beyond just ensuring you get better sleep. Your circadian rhythm is about the complete ebb and flow of your energy throughout the day. There are certain times you're going to be more active and energized, and others you're going to be more mellow. Knowing when these times occur means you can schedule your life to better fit your natural cycles.

People are not machines with uniform, unwavering energy levels no matter the time of day. Firstly, bear in mind that there is nothing innately superior about being a "morning person," and you won't magically be more productive just because you forced yourself to wake up early or get more things done before lunchtime. As we've seen, this advice works for some chronotypes, but not everyone will actually be more productive this way.

The old "early to bed, early to rise" wisdom is not for everyone, in other words. Rather, you need to look at the times when your body is naturally more awake, and make sure you've scheduled your work to coincide with that. It doesn't matter whether this is comfortably done in the morning or almost midnight—if it fits your chronotype and energy levels, it works.

How do you find your "peak hours"? First, become curious about your actual habits over a period of a week. Note the times of day you were most productive. Look for patterns not just in energy levels, but enthusiasm and emotions, too. Look for what inspires energy outbursts, and when you have the most output, work-wise.

Now, the obvious next step is to make sure you're taking advantage of that energy spike by "booking" these peak hours and managing your other less important or less demanding tasks outside that window. Essentially, you are budgeting and managing your energy just as you would your time and money, using what you have most efficiently.

Another way to look at it is by taking the circadian rhythm and extrapolating it into our *ultradian rhythms*, which are the rhythms that move with us through the twenty-four-hour cycle of our lives. Sleep researcher Neil Kleitman identified the presence and importance of rapid eye movement (REM) sleep and discovered that the body generally operates in ninety-minute cycles, moving progressively through periods of higher and lower alertness.

In other words, our energy and alertness come in ninety-minute chunks. These ninety-minute cycles apply whether we are awake or asleep, and we can use this information in a few ways.

First, we now know there is essentially a time limit to energetic and productive thinking. It's not endless; in fact, it might be capped at ninety minutes at a time. At the end of an intense ninety-minute work period, we grow fatigued and begin relying on stress hormones for energy. Then, suffering from overload, the prefrontal cortex begins to shut down, and we move into fight-or-flight mode. We may attempt to override the body's signals by fueling ourselves with caffeine and sugar, but in the end, our focus and concentration suffer.

Additional research from the U.S. Army Research Institute backs up the findings and supports the ninety-minute periods of focus and energy. The point here is to listen to your body. It is telling you exactly how it prefers to function.

Besides creating ninety-minute cycles, the ultradian rhythm also distributes these peaks and dips of energy throughout a twenty-four-hour period in specific ways. There are certain times when you can maximize your thinking, and others when you are setting yourself up for failure. Of course, keep in mind, these are averages, and outliers do exist.

As we move through a typical day, it takes a few hours after waking to reach our peak levels of energy and alertness. For many people, the late morning hours, after 10:00 a.m., represent the highest period of mental sharpness and focus. This is when you might take advantage of your brain functioning at its peak. But remember, you probably have only ninety minutes on average.

Soon after lunch, our energy levels begin to decline.

According to Christopher Barnes's writing in the *Harvard Business Review*, our body's energy naturally dips somewhere between 2:00 and 3:00 p.m., possibly because we are at the midpoint of our wake cycle. For thousands of years, humans have rested during the afternoon (think of the Spanish concept of the midday *siesta* or nap), and only since the Industrial Revolution imposed an emphasis on mass productivity have we begun to eliminate this critical period of rest for the nine-to-five workday.

After we hit that afternoon dip, our energy levels begin rising again, and we generally hit our second peak around 6:00 p.m. As the evening wears on, our energy diminishes, slowly transitioning into sleep cycles.

The ultradian rhythm of energy is something that rules our day-to-day existence. You can fight it, but why would you? Work within the simple guideline it lays out for your energy, and you will find that smarter thinking becomes the rule rather than the exception.

So, we've seen how to tackle and work with sleep, circadian, and ultradian rhythms. Another obvious—but no less critical—aspect to master is your physical well-being. It's easy to imagine we are all just giant heads walking around on stalks, but the fact is that nothing happens in life without the body being in good condition. We all know about the importance of eating a diet that's balanced and optimal for health, but how many of us specifically eat to manage and maintain our energy levels?

Eating for Glucose

Eating for energy consists mainly of focusing on blood sugar levels. You can think of the amount of readily available glucose in your bloodstream as a physiological analogue to "energy"—it's the literal fuel you need to power everything in your body, including the thoughts in your brain. However, there are consequences for having both too much and too little: you know the consequences for too little glucose, but with too much, the body will overcompensate and create a "crash" effect in your energy levels. Keep your blood sugar levels constant and moderate, and the machine of your body will be well-functioning.

The easiest way to start thinking about blood sugar levels is to talk about the glycemic index (GI). The GI is a measure of how quickly your body breaks down different foods, mostly carbohydrates, into glucose. In other words, it measures how much and how quickly a food will affect your blood sugar levels. The higher the GI, the more quickly it evaporates into your bloodstream as glucose.

After a typical meal, your blood sugar level spikes and then insulin is released to regulate it. Your body has ways to keep your blood sugar in a relatively stable range—i.e. releasing stored energy from muscle, liver or fat tissue when blood sugar is low, or releasing insulin to usher excess away when blood sugar is high. When the body detects a large amount of blood sugar, a proportionately large amount of insulin is released, and this is what creates the aforementioned crash effect on energy levels.

Thus, the goal with eating for glucose and abiding by the glycemic index is to try to keep your blood sugar levels as constant as possible. Avoid energy peaks and crashes, and instead cultivate sustained, moderate energy throughout the day. You can do this by understanding timing and food selection.

The lower the GI of a food, the less extreme its effect on the insulin response and the more slowly and steadily it releases sugars into the blood. The result is stable energy levels and appetite. Foods with a higher GI cause the body to release huge spikes of insulin that then clear blood sugar more quickly, leaving you with a "crash" afterwards—one that feels exhausting and can make you hungry all over again. Basically, lower GI foods lead to more stable blood sugar, energy levels, appetite, and mood, while higher GIs can cause us to feel extreme blood sugar and energy fluctuations, plus incite cravings that force us to eat more when we don't need to.

The blood-sugar roller coaster is all about highs and crashes from eating refined carbohydrates and simple sugars. Though GI is not the only feature to look for in a food, it's an important thing to consider with regards to energy. GI says nothing about the caloric value or the nutrient density of a food, so it's worth remembering to use GI as only one factor of many when planning a diet for optimal energy.

Glycemic load (GL) is another measure, and essentially takes into account the *quantity* of carbohydrates you're eating at any time, and the effect this has on your blood sugar. Portion size makes a difference. The higher the glycemic load, the higher the spike in blood sugar levels. Ideally, you want both the GI and GL to be as low as possible. Luckily, the foods with the lowest levels are conveniently the ones that are healthiest in other ways too—i.e., they're packed with vitamins, minerals, fiber, and antioxidants.

There's nothing wrong or unhealthy about carbohydrates per se, but the more refined varieties (i.e. the ones that are immediately converted into glucose) are more likely to lead to unstable blood sugar and the resulting energy spikes and slumps. Fruits and vegetables, after all, are carbohydrates too, but if a food also contains lots of fiber and water, its total glycemic load may be low enough to offset the fact that the bulk of its calories come from simple sugars. So, although things like bananas and potatoes are high-GI foods, they are natural, plant-based foods that still contain plenty of nutrition to outweigh any negative GI effects.

When planning a diet to optimize your energy levels, opt for small amounts of high-quality fats, plenty of protein, and carbohydrates primarily from plant sources. Avoid nutrient-poor refined carbs like cakes and white bread, sugary sweets, soda, white rice, and pasta. If you do decide to have them, try smaller portions and combine them with other low-GI foods so that the total meal's GI is still on the low side. And of course, if you must eat high GI foods, eating them with fat and protein will aid in slowing the glucose absorption.

First, take a look at your diet as it currently is, and figure out the foods you could replace. It can start in a small way. Have wholegrain bread instead of white, bran flakes instead of sugary cereals in the morning, brown rice and other whole grains instead of white, and of course every fruit and vegetable, particularly those that have the highest fiber and water content. There's no need to strictly count carbohydrate grams or be too restrictive about your food choices. Instead, simply get into the habit of choosing the fuel for your body that will "burn the longest" and keep your metabolic fire ticking slowly and steadily, rather than cycling quickly between deathly tired and completely wired up.

Start the day with oatmeal and fruit, some wholegrain toast and peanut butter, or an omelette with veggies. Bran flakes or a smoothie with protein powder are also a great idea. For lunch, try a whole-meal bread sandwich with cheese, smoked salmon, chicken, or a veggie option like hummus. Serve this with a salad, or try a fiber-rich soup or some brown rice with veggies, tofu, or a boiled egg. For dinner, have more of the same or try any meal that's evenly balanced between carbohydrates, fat, and protein—i.e., a protein source like meat or legumes, a carbohydrate source like potato, brown rice, corn or other whole grain, and a fat source like cheese, avocado, nuts or olive oil. Instead of high-GI bombs like ice cream or cake for dessert, try stewed fruit, herbal tea or a few blocks of 75 percent dark chocolate.

Overall, remember that GI isn't the be all and end all of a food; some healthier options will actually have a GI rating higher than the "unhealthier" version, so always use your discretion. Remember, too, that overall GL matters, and that it's OK to have even super-refined carbohydrates on occasion if they're paired with a mostly healthy diet and enjoyed only in small quantities. In the real world, there are many overlapping factors that determine the effect a food will have on blood sugar; GI is simply a guide. However, if you make a point to avoid eating obviously nutrient-poor refined carbs and balance the rest of your meals, you should reap the benefits. You obviously possess enough Internet savvy to purchase this book, so you can easily research "low-GI foods" and build your own meals and substitutions.

One final thing to bear in mind is the *timing* of your meals. A steady, even blood sugar level is maintained if you eat moderately sized meals spaced evenly throughout the day. Though there's some evidence for the health benefits of fasting, the truth is that long periods with low blood sugar, or forcing the body into a ketogenic state (when you are burning your body fat stores for energy, essentially), may be hell on mood and energy levels, even if it does help you shed a few quick pounds. Predictably, when you finally break your fast, insulin will also come rushing out, and a similar energy spike and crash will frequently occur. Opt instead for regularly spaced meals, and avoid letting yourself get famished—this will only mean you have less willpower at the next meal to turn down unhealthy foods.

Though you should watch the *kind* of carbohydrates you eat, there's no point in avoiding them altogether. If you demonize carbs and eliminate them entirely, you may find yourself feeling absolutely starving and grouchy, for no good reason. Carbs are necessary for basic brain function and to power every aspect of your metabolism. Think of carbs as the kindling of your metabolic fire, protein as the structural component to help you repair and maintain your muscles, and fat as essential for energy, but also the proper functioning of your endocrine system and several other important mechanisms in the body.

You don't need to give up drinking fruit juice or never have a donut again, but aim to eat well at least 80 percent of the time, and you'll iron out the bumps on that blood-sugar roller coaster. Vegetables, whole grains, nuts, meat, dairy and eggs will keep you stable and help you get on with the business of life.

Shoring Up Deficiencies

Finally, there's one last way that your diet can help you achieve a more consistently high and stable energy throughout the day: supplements.

A healthy diet is the first step, and indispensable. But there's also a lot you can do to give your body a boost on top of that. We've seen that energy imbalances can come from sleep or ignoring your circadian rhythms, from psychological problems—i.e., stress and trauma—and from physical or mental overexertion—i.e., pushing yourself beyond your natural limits until your body forces you to stop by burning out. But exhaustion, as we've seen, is also about nutrition, and not just on the macro level.

Hidden vitamin and nutrient deficiencies, or even hormonal disturbances can sneakily work to undermine energy levels in the background, even though we're doing our best to sleep well and de-stress.

This is where supplements come in. You might have tried to implement some of the changes mentioned above (that is, getting better sleep, eating low-GI foods) and still find that your focus is weak, your habits are poor, and you generally feel a lack of resilience and enthusiasm for life. Simply not being tired is not quite the same as being energized and wired up for life. If you've tried to relight that fire, and still you feel as though you're merely plodding along, you may need a little something extra.

Supplements play two roles: they can be corrective and address some specific deficiency you have (for example, vitamin D capsules that correct an insufficiency and tackle the cause of your fatigue) or they can be additive, meaning you take them without having any deficiencies, but because you want to enhance your performance, energy or resilience. The latter are called *nootropics*, and could spell the difference between merely chugging along and getting stuck, and actually making your dreams come true.

You could ask your doctor for a blood test if you have persistent fatigue, to help you identify any specific deficiencies. You could also opt for a DIY home test kit that's available in some areas. Common deficiencies leading to fatigue include magnesium, vitamin B-12 (and this is not just for vegans or vegetarians!), iodine, melatonin, vitamin D (especially if you live in a country that gets very dark over the winter) coenzyme Q10, and iron (more common in women).

If your fatigue is persistent, you may be surprised at how much energy can be gained from merely making sure your body is getting the micronutrients it needs. Don't make any assumptions—even those of us who "eat well" can get vitamin and mineral deficiencies, so don't rule this possibility out. As for nootropics, there's a whole world of supplements out there designed to boost performance and well-being—some supported by science, some only with anecdotal evidence. Red panax ginseng, pine pollen, Rhodiola rosea and other "adaptogens" like ashwagandha, turmeric, tulsi (holy basil) and licorice root have all been hailed as great stress-relievers, energy boosters, and general well-being tonics. These are all supplements that have a range of anecdotal and scientific backing—but everyone's body composition is different, so it's best if you perform your own due diligence.

A Note on Water

Was there ever any debate over this? Being dehydrated significantly reduces your energy levels, mental performance, and overall brain health. Our brains are 70 percent water, so it stands to reason they are affected the most when you are in a state of dehydration.

A UK study found that ninety minutes of sweating without additional hydration shrinks the brain as much as a year of aging or almost three months of Alzheimer's Disease (Kempton, 2011). Temporarily, one might hope. Another study suggested that driving while dehydrated can be similar to driving drunk because of the decrease in focus and reaction time, as well as impaired motor skills (Loughborough University, 2012). And there is very little margin for error, as well. Significant detriments to analytical thought, short-term memory, long-term memory recall, problem-solving, and general cognitive performance were found in just a one percent level of dehydration (Riebl, 2013).

Thus, drink more water throughout the day for more energy, and make sure both your body and brain are well-oiled and lubricated. Don't rely on *feeling* thirsty to understand that you need more water. Preempt this, because the thirst response does not activate until you are already dehydrated, and it will be too late by that point. Take a proactive approach to drinking more water and account for weather, environmental conditions, or other factors that would necessitate greater intake. The old maxim of "eight glasses of water a day" may not necessarily be accurate or even necessary, but you probably need more water than you are currently getting.

Drink more water than you think you should and you're on the right track to keeping your body fueled.

Takeaways:

- When we talk about energy, we must start with the physical aspect. Our bodies are our engines, and they must be properly fueled to perform well, or at all. We have to eliminate all of our physical energy vampires and replace them with better habits and awareness. We can take a quick look at what happens when we run out of energy; when we burn out—one of the biggest energy vampires. This is a state of stress and anxiety on the body, where our bodies begin to break down.

- Another prominent energy vampire is a lack of productive and restful sleep. Your sleep hygiene could be terrible and you'd never know it. We should be avoiding blue light before sleeping, lowering stress levels, and keeping a regular sleep schedule. We should also seek to determine our sleep chronotype and understand how it relates to our circadian rhythms. The circadian rhythm directly influences the ultradian rhythm that we abide by when we are awake, and that we take into account with its natural spikes and lulls in energy. Restful sleep is a force multiplier—a quantity that enables great accomplishment in other, unrelated areas.
- Next, we turn to the literal fuel for our bodies, our diets. There is plenty of literature on eating for health, but what about eating for energy? This concerns something that is lesser known: glycemic index (GI) and glycemic load (GL). We want to ensure that our blood sugar levels are constant and moderate, because if levels are too high or too low,

it creates a predictable crash in energy. Thus we must manipulate GI (speed and magnitude of blood sugar from a food) and glycemic load (amount of carbohydrates), as well as timing throughout the day.
- In addition to eating for glucose, we must ensure that we are consuming enough essential vitamins and minerals. We shouldn't be deficient in anything, and we can enhance our energy through specific nootropics, or compounds that give a boost to our physiological states.
- Water is important. Drink more water, hydrate your brain, and keep your energy up.

Chapter 3. Emotional and Mental Energy Vampires

So, the previous chapter takes care of the various ways in which our precious life energy could be faltering or sputtering out in a physical sense. Of course, you may have experienced depleted energy levels even though all the physical boxes seem to be ticked. You could be doing everything right and still feel like your life force is sapped from you. Why?

Remember the energy pyramid? Everything is interrelated. Emotional and mental energy vampires are in some ways worse than their physical counterparts because they're harder to spot and combat. They're ephemeral, and there's no obvious formula of input to output that can fix them. More effort will not equate into a proportionate improvement in energy. No, there's often a root cause that must be addressed, or all your other efforts will be in vain.

It's obvious that you'll be tired if you don't sleep well, but it may not be so obvious that you'll feel utterly exhausted if you've been arguing all morning with a loved one, stressed about money or just carrying around a vague sense of anxiety about life in general. And sometimes, these emotional and mental vampires simply have to run their course, such as waiting for the will to live to return after a painful breakup or divorce.

In fact, many *constantly fatigued* problems come down not to physical issues but rather to emotional and psychological ones (although they can often intertwine and enter into a "chicken or egg" cycle). In the same way a bacteria or virus can weaken your physical body, an emotional "virus" can slow you down too, leaving you feeling depressed, tired, and pessimistic. The mind is more powerful than the body, and it doesn't allow you to forget it.

Consider the phenomenon of psychosomatic illness and people *convincing* themselves into feeling poorly, or those who go completely catatonic overnight because of some unbearably shocking news. Thoughts and emotions can make themselves known in heavy limbs, sluggishness, and feeling as though our life force has been zapped. Have you ever noticed how prone you are to colds and flus when you're stressed, or what worry does to your stomach? Have you noticed how you feel light and healthy around some people and utterly drained around others, as though interacting with them literally sucked the energy out of you?

To add to the matter, many emotional energy vampires are unconscious; the fact that they are manifesting physically is precisely because your conscious mind has not quite figured out a way to acknowledge them. If you have no idea that this is even a problem, you may keep on swallowing supplements and eating your broccoli and diligently getting your eight hours each night, and it won't matter one bit if the thing that's making you tired is a deep dread about your work, or the strain of facing an unpleasant truth.

How you feel about yourself and your place in the world, your deep underlying assumptions about it all—these are all simmering quietly below the surface. If you spent every moment of your life with the unconscious belief, "I'm a failure and I'll never amount to anything," isn't it much the same thing as trying to live with a chronic, low-grade illness?

The Self-Defeating Mind

Emotional energy all starts with the way we view the world and our place in it. Unfortunately, our perception of the world is 99 percent incorrect. There's no other way around it. What we see is often not the reality that exists, and that's completely normal.

This is because of the various biases and perspectives we bring from our past. Some are good; most are negative and the reason we even need to talk about this issue. They are one of the ultimate energy vampires because they shed light on our insecurities and rob us of our confidence and power. We spend so much time worrying and anxious that it leaves us too exhausted to do much else. Any time your brain is in a state of even mild distress, there is energy being discharged for self-protection.

To stop emotional vampires, you must change the way you view the world. Information and events come to us in a neutral state; it is only through our interpretation that these items have positive or negative connotations. How we choose to view events determines our realities and has the ability to completely undermine our confidence and will to persevere.

More than likely, you are suffering from frequent *cognitive distortions*—a view of reality that is negative, pessimistic, and generally incorrect. It can damage your self-esteem, lower your confidence, and make you feel as if you have no control over your life. Cognitive distortion is also a form of self-talk that is damaging, and can become so ingrained and habit-forming that people don't realize they are creating an alternate reality where they are destined for unhappiness and a lack of confidence.

Most of us have enough trouble coping with reality; distorting our view of the world to be more menacing and difficult just saps our confidence and will unnecessarily.

Enter Craig. While returning from the restroom, Craig walked past a closed-door meeting in his supervisor Max's office. As he passed by the glass door, he noticed that almost all his coworkers were in the room, and many glanced in his direction.

He immediately began to feel nervous. Were they talking about him? Had he done something wrong? He was probably going to be fired! Last week, he'd noticed Sheila and Katie giggling and looking at him in the break room. And the Nickerby account had just moved to another company. He was probably going to get fired, and it would be impossible to find another job because he would definitely be getting a horrible recommendation. He wouldn't be able to make his truck payment next month without a job; it would probably get repossessed.

Craig was in a downward spiral for the rest of the day, worrying about his future work prospects and how he would survive without his usual income while looking for a new job. He fretted, worried, and agonized for hours with friends over the phone, which only left him exhausted and stressed and not one step closer to any type of solution.

The next day was Craig's birthday, and he was feeling very depressed. He dragged himself into work, prepared for the worst. He felt it would be fitting to be fired on his birthday (only the fourth worst birthday he would have), and braced for impact.

As soon as he sat down at his desk he heard a loud "Surprise! Happy Birthday, Craig!" All his coworkers were gathered behind his desk, armed with small gifts. Sheila rushed over and blurted out, "We've been planning this surprise for weeks! We thought we had been caught when you walked past Max's office yesterday, but it looks like we really surprised you." Craig was thankful and relieved, but the damage to his energy was already done, and his self-inflicted wounds were all for nothing.

Craig was suffering from severe cognitive distortion.

His perception of an event, a meeting of many of his coworkers, was colored by his negative, draining viewpoint. Although his coworkers were ultimately planning a surprise birthday party, Craig jumped to conclusions and assumed the worst. This cognitive distortion served to lower Craig's self-esteem and put him into a panic mode in which he wasted his energy and time worrying about an unlikely future scenario.

Imagine being at the mercy of these types of distortions and the impact it would have on your energy. The first step to launching a counterattack on these negative thoughts is by noticing when you are having them. Then you must make a conscious effort to turn them off or find alternative explanations for your worries. By refuting or shutting off this negative thinking over and over again, the damaging thoughts will diminish over time and automatically be replaced by more rational, balanced thinking. It is only through constant vigilance that you can replace the bad habit of cognitive distortion with the good habit of positive thinking.

Many of us may notice this type of internal dialogue while at work, but aren't able to recognize that it's something that is disengaging us from reality. Thus, I'll cover a few of the most common cognitive distortions, illustrate them with examples, and discuss how they are detrimental to emotional stability and thus energy.

All-or-Nothing Thinking

- *"Gosh, I haven't read a single book this month and my goal was to read three! I'm horrible at sticking to goals. If I can't read three books, I may as well not read at all."*
- *"I chewed with my mouth open that one time. How could I have done that?! How disgusting. No one will ever be with someone like me. Tasha is going to break up with me tomorrow, I just know it."*

All-or-nothing thinking can also be called tunnel vision. This type of cognitive distortion occurs when you focus only on one outcome or factor to judge an entire situation, and anything else amounts to a failure. Instead of taking a balanced viewpoint, there is only black or white, yes or now, fail or succeed.

As fictional race car driver Ricky Bobby in *Talladega Nights* said, "If you ain't first, you're last." Obviously, this is not true, but that's the stark contrast that this cognitive distortion creates, and it sets you up to feel lousy because failure is the most likely scenario. Not reaching your goal doesn't immediately signal the end of your world as you know it, and consequences that seem enormous and irreversible rarely are.

All-or-nothing thinking also manifests itself through lists of ironclad rules about behavior or expectations. People who break these rules make us feel angry, and in turn, if we break a rule, we feel guilty. Lists of "shoulds" or "musts" such as "I must go to the gym every day" or "I must arrive at work at least fifteen minutes before my shift begins" might sound motivational, but they leave little room for compromise or adjustment if life events get in the way of your plan.

All of these tendencies create a set of expectations that you are destined to fall short of. And when this happens on a continual basis, you can't help but feel inadequate and mediocre at best.

To overcome the cognitive distortion of all-or-nothing thinking, you must challenge yourself to see the middle ground.

Personalizing

- *"Why can't our daughter Marsha hold down a job? She is constantly moving from company to company. I think she was even fired from this last position. I must have done something wrong as a parent. If only we had sent her to Laurelswood High School instead of the public school, this never would have happened! It's all my fault. I should have quit my job and just been there for her."*
- *"I feel terrible that Patricia overcooked the pot roast. If only Jeremy and I hadn't been thirty minutes late for the dinner party. If only I had told him to hurry, this wouldn't have happened! I take full responsibility for this. I should have cooked everything myself."*

Personalization is the mother of guilt. In the cognitive distortion of taking everything personally, you feel responsible for events that cannot conceivably be your fault. While it is admirable to take responsibility for your actions, some things are completely out of your control: the subway schedule, other people's actions, and a million day-to-day factors.

While engaging in personalizing, you might believe that everything others say or do is a direct personal reaction to you even when logically this doesn't fit. It's pretty difficult to feel good about yourself if you believe you are responsible for all the ills of the world around you. To be confident you have to be able to focus on yourself, not on the perceived reactions of others.

The opposite of personalizing is *externalizing*. It is another important cognitive distortion to note. When caught in this trap, individuals refuse to blame themselves for anything; instead, they blame everyone and everything else. The world is out to get them, and only them. These individuals blame others for holding them back, causing them pain or sadness, and even point to other people as the cause of life troubles. All of this blame is given without any recognition for the part the individual played in his or her own troubles, pain, or sadness. Neither of these types of thinking are healthy, and they both force you to expend a considerable amount of emotional energy jumping through hoops and agonizing over everyday issues.

In order to escape from both of these cognitive distortions, question what part you actually played in the event and consider options in which you are not entirely to blame.

Overgeneralization

- *"I'm never going to find a girlfriend because my last date went so terribly. I am destined to be single forever."*
- *"He will never be on time. He was late for both of our previous meetings. He's a lost cause. I am not going to meet with him again."*

In the trap of *overgeneralization,* you take one small negative experience and assume all similar future experiences will be negative. Overgeneralization is unrepresentative of reality because you are operating on minimal experience, information, and evidence. You are jumping to conclusions and constructing a world that doesn't exist in reality; it is truly an exercise in imagination (a classic sneaky energy drainer).

Common cues of overgeneralization are "always" and "never." When starting a sentence or a thought with "always" or "never," consider whether you have the experience or evidence to back up the statement. Do you have the ability to look past your current feelings or the most recent event that is causing you to feel this way? The very nature of emotions is to overwhelm and cloud judgment—perhaps you are merely honoring your emotions instead of seeking a balanced view.

To overcome the trap of overgeneralization, take time to question whether evidence may exist showing that future events could be different. Consider just how little information you have. Has every event of this type in your life ended in exactly the same way, or are there more than a few outliers? Do all of your friends have the exact same story, or have some of them had different experiences?

Catastrophizing

- *"Lacy is out late again. I just know that she's cheating on me! We're never going to last as a couple; we have to be heading for divorce. I need to call a lawyer right now."*
- *"Why haven't I received a letter from the University of California yet? They must be rejecting me. I can't believe it! I'm not going to get into any universities. What am I going to do? I guess I need to start learning how to become a plumber."*

When you engage in *catastrophizing*, you immediately jump to the worst-case scenario and lose hope because the event seems so imminent. Catastrophizing can cause you to become stressed and anxious. Even the smallest actions can have enormous consequences. How stable and energetic can you really be if every day you appear to be facing your own personal version of the apocalypse?

As with other cognitive distortions, a degree of introspection and thinking about your thoughts is necessary. Slow down and question whether things are truly as bad as you are making them seem. Are your assumptions even realistic? Consider alternative explanations and past experiences in similar situations.

Ask yourself: In past similar situations, what did I do and how did the event turn out? How would an innocent bystander explain the situation? What am I fixating on and why?

Jumping to Conclusions

- *"Why didn't David smile back at me this morning? He must think the project proposal I sent him yesterday afternoon is stupid!"*
- *"There's no point in even going to the gym. I'm never going to reach my goal of running that 10k with Candace."*

Jumping to conclusions occurs when you make an irrational assumption about people or circumstances based on personal opinion and feeling. It begins with feelings of inadequacy or insecurity which influence the way you perceive events and statements. When you observe something that supports your worst fears, you take it as a confirmation of everything you secretly knew to be terrible and true. Just like with other cognitive distortions, it causes you to fall down a rabbit hole of negativity until you end up at the worst possible conclusion.

There are two categories within the cognitive distortion of jumping to conclusions: *mind-reading* and *fortune-telling*. While engaging in mind-reading, you assume you know what someone else is thinking. It is impossible to know exactly what someone else is thinking, yet with this cognitive distortion, people make decisions based on the imagined thoughts of other people. And of course, you assume people are always thinking the worst about you.

Fortune-telling involves predicting negative future events without evidence. When engaging in fortune-telling, you predict only negative outcomes for the future and have no real basis for doing so. Fortune-telling makes any semblance of optimism impossible.

Emotional Reasoning

- *"I can't afford to pay all of my bills again this month. I feel hopeless and depressed. There is no solution to my problems."*
- *"Oh my gosh, why did I bring up that movie!? It's ten years old; everyone will think I'm so out of touch. I'm such a bore at all these parties."*

Engaging in the cognitive distortion of emotional reasoning means that you are taking your emotions as evidence. Whatever you feel right now is whatever reality you find yourself in. That's a difficult way to live.

While engaging in this behavior, observed evidence is discarded in favor of the "truth" of your feelings about the event. Humans tend to believe that how they feel must automatically be true. If you feel stupid and boring, then you must actually be stupid and boring. This is commonly referenced by the phrase "I feel it; therefore, it must be true."

Emotional reasoning is one of the most dangerous of the cognitive distortions because it can be so wildly different from reality and in the span of minutes can change. Is reality actually shifting moment by moment? Of course not! Only your emotions are changing that quickly.

Being conscious of and allowing yourself to feel your emotions is important to maintaining your emotional health and energy; however, that does not mean you should take your emotions to heart as a true expression of reality. In fact, your emotions often have very little to do with the status quo of reality. Remember, reality is neutral, yet your emotions cause you to perceive reality as either positive or negative.

To escape the trap of emotional reasoning and take control of this "automatic response," question whether your emotional state of mind is preventing you from viewing events clearly. Ask yourself what the objective bystander interpretation would be, compare it to your emotional response, and try to mediate the difference. Just like you wouldn't go grocery shopping when hungry, you shouldn't evaluate anything when emotional. Always take time to return to a calm state before making decisions or committing yourself to a specific course of action.

Viewing a situation while emotional, or with emotional reasoning, is like watching a completely neutral scene with horror music being played over it. And then joyous music. And then the next minute, music fitting for a clown's entrance. You won't know what's really happening in front of your face because the music will influence you a certain way.

Damaging Comparisons

Finally, although not a true cognitive distortion, viewing life through comparisons with others has the same tendency to create a negative reality while wasting an unhealthy amount of energy on something you cannot change.

Regardless of whatever strengths and qualities you bring to the table, you will become miserable when you compare yourself to others. We have a tendency to compare ourselves to other people around us or to some kind of imagined ideal—and neither of these situations is good.

Comparing is a learned habit that destroys your confidence because it tries to put all your value and worth into one tiny aspect. You have to understand that you are a compilation of many different traits and talents. You have your appearance, your earning ability, your ability to play sports, how fast you type, and so on. These all matter.

Unfortunately, when we measure ourselves against others, we ignore or throw out all the things we are good at and only focus on the one thing we're not good at or that we imagine others excel at. The problem with comparing in a social setting is that we often carry with us a fictionalized ideal of how a "perfect" person would get along in particular social situations.

This person is about as real as Superman. Unfortunately, we treat that notion as if it's absolutely real, and we allow ourselves to feel crappy and inferior when we don't measure up. When we compare ourselves to this imagined ideal, we fail to see our strengths, value, and worth.

When you compare, you only see what's on the outside, what people allow others to see about them. But what you're viewing isn't the whole picture, and is not necessarily who these other people really are—it's just their very best version of themselves, the one they are willing to present to the world. You end up degrading yourself by choosing your darkest and worst view of yourself to compare.

Other people aren't only what they show to the world. Most people put on a good show. You probably know a couple that appears to get along great and be very much in love. They seem totally happy and as if they truly connect with each other in an enviable way. But do you really know what might be going on in their private life?

Hopefully you can understand that these distortions are not only falsehoods, but enormous wastes of our mental and emotional energy. The more time we spend in our own heads agonizing about the possibilities of our internal world, the less energy we can expend toward the external world.

Challenging Beliefs

Unfortunately, these cognitive distortions reflect our core beliefs and are part of our personal psychological networks. They're instilled at an early age and reinforced by our experiences. Many of us have been trained to waste emotional energy catering to these distortions. That's why they're hard to nail down—they are how you view the world, and don't require conscious effort. And yet, we still feel their effects on us through triggering events and emotional distress. An ungodly amount of energy is squandered here.

Challenging and changing distortions from an analytical perspective is what is known as *cognitive behavioral therapy*, or CBT for short. The main strategy of CBT is to teach people how to deal with their negative core beliefs, head-on, and reprogram them into something less harmful.

There are two primary methods for intervention in the cycle of low confidence. The first is *cognitive restructuring*—a technique for identifying negative cognitive patterns and untrue assumptions we make about ourselves and altering them.

Cognitive restructuring is a treatment intended to show people why they are stuck in these negative feedback loops and what they can do to significantly alter their thought and behavior patterns in order to remove themselves from the vicious cycle. By recognizing a negative thought pattern and understanding why it persists, we can react differently to it and steer ourselves in a positive direction.

How does one build their awareness about their counterproductive thoughts, emotions, and behaviors? Generally, the first step of those methods entails identifying subconscious thoughts—the ones providing us with a continuous commentary on our experiences as we are living them. These thoughts are constantly affecting our moods because we tend to simply accept them as accurate reflections of reality and ourselves.

When we stop accepting the narrative being written by our subconscious, we are able to consider alternative points of view. Suddenly the cycle is broken, or at least altered. This shift leads to a more sensible and stable way of thinking about whatever is causing us distress at any given time, preventing us from falling into those vicious cycles mentioned earlier.

By simply considering alternative possibilities, we can balance out our emotions and thoughts and reduce the sadness and hopelessness that occurs when we get trapped in a negative feedback loop. This, in turn, enables us to engage in behaviors and activities which promote our well-being, pulling us out of our dark mindset and making us stronger and better.

Few people are actively aware of their thinking patterns, even though they engage in these patterns every day. CBT allows you to address errors in your thinking to correct your behavior and in turn change your life. You might assume that you require a therapist, or at least an incredibly patient friend to conduct CBT, but that's where thought diaries and worksheets come into play.

The concept of the thought diary was borne from the desire to identify the core beliefs that inform our actions and emotions. It uncovers the relationships between our behavior, thoughts and feelings. Basically, it's the process of cognitive behavioral therapy, and similar to how a counselor might help one get to the root of their psychological issues.

A typical entry in a thought diary outlines a triggering event or thought, the self-messaging that comes from it, and the resultant emotions that emerge. Sifting through all this information brings up your core beliefs so you can challenge them. Remember, we want to try to isolate and analyze the automatic thoughts we have, and replace them with healthier versions.

Steps in a thought diary entry can be arranged in the easy-to-remember A-B-C format—although for the purposes of this process it's actually A-C-B:

Activating Event. This is simply the origin point of your emotional change. It could be an actual, physical event. But it could also be an internal event—a thought, memory or mental image. It's whatever caused your emotional status to change from calm to agitation:

- Hearing an old song that reminds you of someone you were close to
- Running into an old friend on the street
- Being criticized by a supervisor
- Remembering being bullied by a high school classmate

Consequences. In this step you identify the specific emotions and sensations that arose. Start with the most basic of emotions—sad, glad, mad, and scared—and then branch out. These could be simple feeling words—"anxious," "unhappy," "sickened," "panicky," "melancholy," "confused," and so forth. To get more specific about the emotions involved, you may want to rate how intensely you felt them on whatever scale works for you. Maybe you were 65 percent panicky and 35 percent confused. Your feelings of sickness may have been a ten, and your anxiety may have been a five.

Underline or circle which emotion was most relevant.

Beliefs. This is where the action begins. How do you link the activating event with the consequences? What unconscious narrative or story did you tell yourself to achieve the consequence? What leaps in logic or to conclusions did you make to arrive at your current negative state? Getting to the bottom of these beliefs involves some drilling of yourself with progressive questioning, until you finally get to the root of your situation—your core beliefs:

- "What was I thinking?"
- "What was going through my head when this happened?"
- "What's wrong with that?"
- "What does this all mean?"
- "What does it reveal about me?"

Yes, it's a lot of work, and you might struggle at points to obtain the answers you're looking for. But the effort to peel away layers of self-messaging will eventually pay off. When your investigation finally brings you face-to-face with your core beliefs, that's when you can start the process of challenging them.

Let's take an example of seemingly benign activating events and put them through the ABC ringer. They may seem a bit abbreviated, but you'll find that they closely mirror real-life situations.

1. Steve is having a conversation with his new friend Emily at table at a bar. They're having a good talk, until Steve's acquaintance Jack walks up, pulls up a chair, and starts chatting, oblivious to the fact that he stopped Steve and Emily's conversation cold. Steve is angry. You won't like him when he is angry.

Steve's activating event is Jack stopping his conversation. That's easy.

What is the consequence—what did this event activate, feelings-wise? Steve felt flustered, for one. That was probably the dominant emotion. He'd give it an "8" on a scale of 1 to 10. He also sensed anger and frustration, but not quite as powerfully as the panic. Maybe a "4." He felt the front of his head get a little heavy. Steve qualifies that as "confusion." But he's not sure why, so he gives this a "3."

Now Steve has to figure out why this particular event made him freak out. What is the connection from the action to the consequential emotional state? Does he dislike Jack? No, not at all, he decides. He's an okay guy, if sometimes a little overexcitable.

So, Steve asks himself what was going through his head at the time. He was having a good conversation with Emily, feeling like they were both talking earnestly and actively about shared interests. And then it got interrupted. He felt flustered.

Why? Because he was disappointed that the conversation was derailed, and that Jack wasn't self-aware enough to know he was interrupting.

What does that mean? He feels that Jack was being careless about his ego and personality and thought nothing of imposing his will over Steve's.

Why is that? Because Steve doesn't think he asserts himself enough.

And why is that? Because Steve believes he's too modest to ever be able to speak up for himself.

And what does that mean? Steve doesn't feel he deserves respect, and Jack's interruption was just a reminder that he isn't worthy of it.

That's Steve's core belief: He has little if any self-regard and thinks he lets people take advantage of his recessive nature to "bowl him over" and take over in social situations, without regard to what he really wants. Because of that, he doesn't see himself as somebody respectable. It's not easy to reach this point just from analyzing a reaction to an interruption, but doing so is how you come to understand and change your core beliefs.

Challenging beliefs does have the temporary effect of requiring even more of your emotional and mental energy, but this will ultimately decrease the ways in which your brain runs itself in exhausting circles.

The *Real* Vampires

Negative thoughts, beliefs, and feelings about yourself are not the only emotional energy vampires you need to watch out for. There are also more literal "vampires," i.e. people who work to undermine your emotional and psychological health by draining away your energy, optimism, and well-being. Now, this is not to say there are purely "bad" people out there who are responsible for all our negative feelings when we are around them. After all, every one of us has at some point been negative, unreasonable, and difficult to deal with.

Rather, learning to spot and avoid or manage negativity in others is more about self-care and preserving and maintaining your own energy. It's a little like keeping your distance from someone who's coughing and sneezing, or ensuring you don't make yourself a target for someone's bad day or emotional outburst.

Anyone who has spent even a tiny amount of time or energy on personal development will at some point come to the problem of what to do with people who don't share your enthusiasm for growing and evolving. If you're battling mental illness, trying to be a better person or simply attempting to get more joy, creativity, and meaning out of your life, you may be stumped about what to do when you encounter people who seem hell-bent on being negative, judgmental and, well, generally awful.

Humans are social creatures, and even for those of us who feel like we're independent, the emotions, attitudes, and words of others can have a profound effect on our own moods and the way we see ourselves. You could work incredibly hard to cultivate a healthy sense of self-esteem, and progress immensely in this goal, only to have a rude, critical person tear it all down with, "Oh, you're wearing *that*?" So much personal development focuses on what we can do with our own thoughts, feelings and beliefs. But learning to contend with *other people's* negativity is just as important.

Firstly, learn to spot personality traits that seek to bring others down, or lower the "energy" of every interaction or conversation. Look for those people that are always complaining or whining, never have a positive word to say about themselves or others, and constantly seem to be the victim of some person or circumstance. These people are passive, expect the worst and always go for the worst interpretation, including being chronically insulted or disappointed with things around them.

Though they are quick to find fault with literally everything, such a person may nevertheless hardly think to ask if they're in the wrong, because they simply never are. Granted, we've all had people we don't get on with, but a true "energy vampire" will have a consistently negative pattern with *everyone* they meet, not just you. They'll have a reputation for being joyless, difficult to please, judgmental, or drama causing. They're most familiar with anger and dissatisfaction, but you never see them express love or gratitude. In fact, even when something good happens to this person, they'll find something wrong with it and dwell on that instead, making sure everyone around them knows how unhappy they are.

When you're with a person like this you feel drained, to put it simply. You may feel like they're constantly manipulating you, judging you, framing you as the bad guy, or turning every happy thought or impulse into the worst-case scenario. It's exhausting. They may argue all the time, subtly insult you or undermine you, or just generally be depressing to be around.

The trouble with a person like this is that over time that negative attitude starts to rub off. Whenever you are upbeat, their bad mood seems to win out, and you find yourself drawn into complaining sessions instead. Maybe you felt really good about something...until you told this person. You may start to buy into their way of thinking, really believing that everything is terrible and nothing can be done about it. Rather than brainstorming solutions or options, this person constantly focuses on the problem, resorting to impotent complaining or blaming someone else.

Be careful with a person like this, since their negativity can become a self-fulfilling prophesy. Their intense focus on the negative may mean they never amount to much in life, systematically creating more pessimism all around them. You yourself can become sucked in and become part of this attitude of negativity.

It's easy to see these characteristics in some people, but harder in others. Do you know anyone who has convinced everyone around them that life is just harder for them, that they're the perpetual victim and it's everyone else's fault? People like this can be so good at twisting things that their entire surrounding network buys into the same negative narrative. Be wary of people who always seem to be in one kind of crisis or another, who want to draw you into arguments or otherwise position you as an actor in their play.

People who cannot admit mistakes, appreciate the things they have or seek solutions to their problems will never grow. If you're trying to grow yourself—emotionally, spiritually, financially—a person with this mindset will only work against you. Don't spend time and effort building up your own store of emotional strength and energy only to have someone else sap it right out of you.

So how do you deal with someone like this, especially if you work together or they're a family member? The first thing to do is to become crystal clear on your boundaries. Do the opposite of a toxic vampire and keep yourself in a proactive, optimistic frame of mind: nobody can force you to do anything, and you are not required to expose yourself to someone else's negativity.

Become aware in yourself of your own personal limits. We can all tolerate some negativity in other people—otherwise we wouldn't be able to help those in genuine need!—but take the time to ask what your tolerance level is and establish a boundary that will not be violated. Walk away. Politely change the topic. Opt out of conversations that only serve to suck the optimism out of you. Recognize when someone's negativity is intruding on your own peace of mind, and then calmly but assertively change the situation or remove yourself from it. It may be difficult or awkward to deliberately step out of someone else's misery game, but you deserve to be around people who support and build you up.

Of course, this is easier said than done. It's easy to walk away from negativity if it comes from a colleague you don't encounter much at work, or someone just passing through your life. But what if the negative person is your spouse, your child or a dear friend of many years? It can be difficult to draw boundaries when someone you care about is so clearly suffering and in distress. What do you do then?

First, realize that even though we all wish it wasn't the case, we are all responsible for our own emotional well-being, and nobody can *make* anyone else happy on their behalf. Get crystal clear on this point: compassion and care can go a long way, but if someone is not ready to accept that help or compassion, we only hurt ourselves in trying to rush in to solve the problem for them. Maintaining your own boundaries whilst acting with compassion can be tricky, but it is more than possible.

Be generous in caring gestures that don't drain you or cost you anything: give the person in need a hug, a compliment, or share a nice memory. One of the best things you can do for people trapped in negativity is to model optimism—let your own light shine and simply share a smile, even if they're being down on themselves or on you. They may not show it at the time, but your enthusiasm and attitude may well shift something in them, or inspire them. Try to show unconditional respect, even if they're difficult with you. When you praise them or give them a compliment, make it about something fundamental; i.e., try to affirm their worth as a human being no matter what. Make them feel welcome and appreciated, and make it clear that even though you're setting a boundary, you love and care for them and want to encourage their happiness.

You can make suggestions or offer advice, but don't take it personally if they don't accept it. Just be there to listen. Try not to get embroiled in the details of what they're feeling negative about—rather, be a positive force and support them, without supporting their negativity. Finally, be ready to reinforce your boundaries when necessary. Being sympathetic and understanding with loved ones adds immense meaning to life. But it's never worth sacrificing our own hard-won peace of mind, and in any case, we don't help a negative person by becoming just as negative as they are!

Keep an eye on your own emotional state. Be vigilant about the temptation to make others' problems your own, or to assume that you're responsible for them somehow. Have empathy without guilt. Give support and a kind ear, but don't mistake your help for getting involved in their drama directly. Respect that everyone is on their own journey in life, and as much as we care, some people will take paths that make them unhappy. Don't judge, don't try to save them; just be there and show presence and compassion. Then, get on with your own life—the only thing you can realistically control is your own attitude.

As you get better at maintaining your own state of mind despite others' negativity, you'll naturally gravitate toward those that *are* better aligned with you and your vision. Cultivate a positive energy and you will find yourself more attracted to (and more attractive to!) other people with similar attitudes. Seek out those people who fill you with energy, and who leave you feeling more inspired and joyful than you were before. There are people who will understand, support and encourage you. Find those people, and develop strong ties with them. Rather than drain you, these are the people who will feed your happiness and success in life.

Whether it's at home, at work or in your community at large, a network of like-minded, supportive people can feed off of each other's positive energy and create wonderful things together. Lift others up, praise those around you and support others, and you'll attract others who will do the same. Have gratitude for yourself and others, take responsibility and be proactive. Just like physical energy, emotional energy can feed on itself; the more you cultivate it in your life, the more of it there is, and the easier it is to create more. This is why it's so important to take care when dealing with people who undermine that energy, while simultaneously fostering and developing relationships with those people who *give* you energy.

Occasionally, we all have to take the difficult step of cutting out people entirely if they're toxic and refuse our help. Do this with kindness and compassion, and without guilt. When people are ready to evolve, they will, and not a moment before. All you ultimately have power to change is yourself. So, focus on that.

The Exhausted Mind

We now move to *mental* energy vampires. These can sometimes be confused or combined with emotional energy vampires, though it's ultimately not so important which category your vampire falls into. Mental energy is about the load on our brains and fighting our way back from overwhelm, whereas emotional energy is about how about we feel about ourselves and the world. Mental energy is what we're lacking when we're physically fit, emotionally stable, yet utterly unable to have a coherent or analytical thought.

Surprisingly, we can experience a drained brain quite easily.

The prefrontal cortex, where our higher thinking resides, is like a calf muscle that grows tired and eventually stops working in the correct way. Our brains have a limited number of thoughts and decisions we can meaningfully analyze and make, and the more decisions we consider, the more fatigued we get. This is a phenomenon more generally known as *ego depletion*.

Ego depletion is the idea that our mental resources are limited. When our resources drain or decrease, our mental activities go poorly. This phenomenon was first discovered in relation to self-control, where experiments (Baumeister et al., 1998) showed that subjects who resisted chocolate performed worse and gave up earlier on a puzzle task. In other words, ego depletion was in full effect, and the amount of self-control they exhibited in resisting the chocolate directly weakened their ability to persist with the puzzle task.

Self-discipline and decision quality decreased quickly as ego depletion started to take place. If you're thinking you've read something recently that claims the concept of ego depletion has come into doubt in recent years, that's true, and we'll discuss that at the end of this section.

Once you get over the initial surprise that something as small as making a decision can deplete your mental resources, you begin to find that it makes all too much sense. The brain requires energy to act and think. In fact, the brain uses up to 20 percent of our daily energy consumption, despite being only 2 percent of the mass of our bodies. Each conscious thought, decision, and task requires a certain amount of activation energy.

The thought process involved in the debate of overindulging in chocolate or not can be quite lengthy and agonizing, and as the experiment showed, it can eliminate your capacity for self-control in the future. It's easy to resist chocolate once or twice, but when you encounter the temptation repeatedly throughout the day, your self-control will likely erode, and it will become nearly impossible to say no—because your brain will run out of juice to do so.

Further support for the theory of ego depletion came in the form of feeding versus starving the brain and then seeing what happened while using self-control.

Experiments showed that using self-control depleted the brain of glucose, its primary energy source, and that ingesting sources of nutrition and glucose could reverse ego depletion and energize people's sense of discipline and self-control. Self-control uses a significant amount of your brain's power reserves, and purely exercising self-control can make you function noticeably less efficiently overall.

Our mental energy can be drained all too easily, so the question is how to safeguard this reservoir of brainpower for when you need it. How can you keep yourself energized and charged as often as possible?

Start by viewing your energy as a battery with a low charge. How would you protect your smartphone's battery if you knew you were going to be watching three hours of video on it later? Decision-making, motivating, and using self-control all draw from the same pool of the prefrontal cortex, so these are the activities you need to be mindful of.

You should try to get a sense of what is trivial in your day in terms of motivation, decisions, or self-discipline—and remove or avoid these elements.

How do you know if something is trivial? If it's truly trivial, it won't matter if you ignore it, or the choices you make will have no ill effect that lasts longer than a few minutes. This is a tough step for most of us because we are trained to give our full and undivided attention to something, lest we perform it poorly. In a way, this point advocates simply seeing what you can get away with paying little attention to—for your prefrontal cortex's sake. Every percentage of your battery you save for that task later makes a difference.

Trivial decisions should only be allocated a trivial amount of mental bandwidth, so try to keep things proportional so you can preserve as much as possible for when you need it. If something doesn't impact your life, take it off your plate as soon as possible.

The overall aim of this point is to make fewer conscious choices per day. Instead of even dealing with some decisions, you could choose to automate them—in other words, pick only one option and stick with it for consistency and ease. In a sense, you are making rules for yourself to eliminate options—for instance, one lunch, one outfit, one music playlist, and one method of doing things.

This is also the purported reason Apple founder Steve Jobs had a standard uniform of sneakers, a black turtleneck, and comfortable jeans. It was so he could avoid making decisions and save his brainpower for when he actually needed it. On a daily basis, this can truly transform into energy you can use for maximum discipline and motivation.

Your mental resources always recharge, but they are easily depleted. Get into battle mode and treat your brain like a muscle that you need for peak energy.

As mentioned earlier, there has been doubt cast on ego depletion in recent years as a scientific theory. Some follow-up studies have found inconclusive results based on Baumeister's work, and others have determined that ego depletion only occurred when the participants already knew about the theory prior to being studied—it gives people an easy excuse to give up on things, as a result of "being drained."

Ego depletion may not be conclusively proven, but we can still make a credible argument that consciously having to think about ten tasks in a day is more mentally strenuous than thinking about two tasks in a day. The more you have to think about, the less energy you will be able to muster up. The argument for lessening the load on the prefrontal cortex remains the same; the term just changes slightly from ego depletion to overall energy depletion.

Based on what we've just learned about the brain and its tendency to quickly be exhausted, we can say it is just like any other part of your body in that it needs to be taken care of physically. We know that if your brain is deprived of nutrition and the proper amount of sleep, it will cease to function well and be drained of energy.

But after having fulfilled those foundational requirements, stress is one of the biggest and most insidious influences on the brain's health.

If you want a clear and concrete illustration, you don't have to look any further than any veteran or trauma victim suffering from post-traumatic stress disorder (PTSD) and how their lives are negatively affected. They literally lack the ability to function in daily life because they are so tense, and they are likely to snap at any given moment as a release for their anxiety and fear. All their energy is devoted to emergency alarm systems, and this constant drain leaves them unable to think beyond the current moment.

A plethora of research has found that stress impacts the brain's health and mental capacity in hugely negative ways. This is in large part due to the body's physiological response to stress. But first, it will be helpful to define the difference between the two main types of stress: chronic and acute stress.

Chronic stress is when you are under ongoing stress for a relatively long period of time—something as small as being under a constant heavy load at work or dealing with a relationship that is frequently combative. These are small sources of stress that seem insignificant until you look at the cumulative effects and realize you are always on edge, testy, and tense with knots in your shoulders. When we are experiencing chronic stress (the amount of which is highly variable and relative to the person's tolerance), our body is in a state of physiological arousal. This is known as the fight-or-flight response, and it's our body's main defense mechanism when it senses a stressor.

This response was useful millennia ago when the terms "fight" and "flight" were taken literally—if the body sensed a stressor or a reason to be in fear, it would put itself on the highest levels of alertness and be prepared for a fight to the death, if necessary, or for running away as quickly as possible. In either case, the body's hormones, heart rate, and blood pressure are highly elevated. The main stress hormone, cortisol, is released in spades and has been implicated in causing the state of alertness.

So if you are under chronic stress, you are permanently in this fight-or-flight mode of alertness and have an excess of cortisol. Your body will very rarely reach the relaxation phase, which is known as a state of homeostasis. And unfortunately, cortisol saps your energy and leaves you exhausted.

Chronic stress makes you alert and physiologically aroused *all the time*. This is exhausting both physically and mentally and has the effect of shrinking your brain. Studies have shown that chronic stress has caused as big as a 14 percent decrease in hippocampal volume (the area of your brain responsible for memory encoding and storage), which is startling. When we're stressed, we're also more prone to emotional outbursts, unhealthy thought patterns, and even poor digestion and sleep.

A study (Pasquali, 2006) showed that memory in rats was negatively affected when the rats were exposed to cats, which presumably caused stress. The rats that were exposed to cats far more routinely were unable to locate certain entrances and exits.

The difficult part is you may not realize you are under chronic stress, because it has become normalized for you. It is just like when your shoulders tense up—you probably don't recognize it until someone points it out, and you can see the contrast between being relaxed and being tense.

The cumulative effects of being constantly on edge, paranoid, unable to focus, and feeling despair and overwhelm will catch up to you. Imagine being pumped up on adrenaline for days, weeks, or months. Not only will it impair your memory and brain processing, but it will leave you unable to function in general. Excess and consistent cortisol can cause a loss of neurons in the prefrontal cortex and hippocampus, as well as decrease the neurotransmitter serotonin, which is what creates the feeling of *happiness*. This is what people with PTSD suffer, but to a much higher degree.

Acute stress, on the other hand, is not something that will slide by unnoticed.

Acute stress is the sudden jolt of adrenaline you experience when someone cuts you off in traffic and you nearly crash, or when you get into a heated argument. However, acute stress is momentary, temporary, and you can feel it and notice it. This is when adrenaline is coursing through your veins, leaving your palms sweaty and hands shaking. Your body is trying to give you the alertness and strength you need for any response. Intense bouts of acute stress can even cause headaches, muscle tension, upset stomach, or vomiting.

If this stress persists and lasts for a longer period of time, it just may cross the threshold into chronic stress.

But the labels are unimportant. What's important is what happens to your brain's abilities and energy levels when you are under any type of stress. The brain literally rewires to be more efficient in conducting information through the circuits that are most frequently activated. When stress is frequent, these pathways can grow so strong that they become your brain's default route to its lower, reactive control centers. Your primitive brain dominates more frequently, and you lose touch with your conscious, logical, and calm brain.

We can't simply plan to avoid stressful situations in our life, nor can we eliminate the vampiric people we described earlier. The best we can do is try and safeguard ourselves, but our efforts will never be foolproof. Life is simply not that predictable or full of choices for most of us. The much better approach is to develop tools to cope with stress, and that's where we move next.

Keeping Calm

A calm mind is an energetic mind. We turn to the practice of mindfulness to relax the brain and make it so that your natural state of mind is rational, nonreactive, and in energy conservation mode.

Mindfulness is the practice of purposefully focusing all your attention on the current moment and being completely aware of yourself, your emotions, and your thoughts.

It can keep your mind from overthinking and running amok, which is the precursor to drained mental energy. The person who is aware of their thoughts as they are happening is far more likely to keep it together and calm versus the person who is unaware of what is happening in the present moment.

You might be consumed by thoughts of past regrets or by anxiety about a future that may never occur. Being in these states makes it easy to slip. It's not so much that donuts will appear in your mouth if you're unaware and distracted, but you won't properly be able to assess whether you are thinking with your primal or logical brain.

In some sense, this factor is going to be our biggest enemy to a stressed and exhausted mind. Our brains are working against us, but the lives we lead are as well. Most of us face constant stress and anxiety in varying degrees. It doesn't have to be debilitating to cause damage over time; it simply has to take us off the path of presence and emotional stability.

Mindfulness is a handy solution to all of those problems. It can both recharge you, and insulate you from the stresses of the exterior world. As mentioned, it is quite literally the practice of emptying your mind—most frequently by focusing on your breathing, for example. Of course, it is difficult to let go of thoughts and concerns because you feel that you must ensure they don't fall through the cracks. The two worst things you can do for yourself are focusing on past events that you can't change, or zeroing in on present events and comparing them with your future. One is long gone, and one has yet to happen. Neither should be your concern.

Practicing mindfulness will feel distressing at first because people who are stressed or overwhelmed constantly feel that they have too much on their plate to ever stop churning. This makes everything worse; when you're continuously moving 24/7, this gives your brain and body very little time to recharge. As we've mentioned at various points in this book, a stressed brain is the opposite of an energetic brain.

Let go of the past, the future. One doesn't exist anymore, and the other may never come to be. Spending your time thinking about them is the definition of useless. And—you guessed it—a massive waste of energy because there's nothing to be done about them. Even attempt to drop what your thoughts and feelings are bound by in the present moment. Anything you can potentially be distracted by, just drop it and trust that it will be right where you left it in thirty minutes. As a last resort, make a list of these thoughts before you attempt to achieve mindfulness, and rest assured that the world will not end in the meantime.

Your focus should be only on what is happening now in your physical surroundings. Let go of what might happen later, what happened earlier, and all thoughts of the present. The only thing that matters is your breathing, your physical sensations, and the noises, sounds, smells, and sights around you.

Although it is most common to sit during meditation, you may choose to kneel or stand. Just make sure that whatever option you pick is comfortable for you to remain for thirty minutes. You can't empty your mind if your body is suffering. Ease yourself from any tension you might feel by relaxing your body as a whole and focusing your mind on the task at hand—*nothingness*.

Make sure you aren't bent over so that the air you breathe is easily accessible to your lungs. Inhale through your nose. Ensure that your breaths are deep and slow. In doing so, you will allow the air you take in to go directly to your stomach, breathing the correct way for the purposes of your meditation practice.

Your mind may begin to wander from your breath, but don't chastise yourself—this is only natural. When wandering takes place, forgive, forget, move forward, and focus on your breathing. This will help you regain focus rather than wrestle with your wayward thoughts. You'll notice how easy it is for your anxieties to hijack your peace of mind and constantly jump into the mental space you've created. Instead of engaging with them and unfolding these thoughts, observe them and just let them go, then return to your breathing. We're not necessarily trying to quiet our minds, but rather focus all our chatter onto one thing.

For some of us with noisier minds, you might find it more helpful to focus on a physical sensation. For instance, some will balance a cup of water on their heads (or simply hold it) because this is an act that requires the utmost concentration.

Coincidentally, this is why many feel that running and other repetitive motions can create a meditative state. You can also move through your body, limb by limb, and feel the sensations present in each part.

Let go. Enjoy the break from the outside pressures you face daily. Reboot your brain and eliminate all the clutter that was preventing you from thinking clearly or being self-aware. Think about how the air feels on your lips, in your nose, and down your throat. Focus on the sound of inhalation and exhalation.

If it sounds too simplistic to be effective, you're in for a surprise. At the core, this is where mindfulness comes from. Your brain gains a rare reprieve from its efforts as the proverbial mouse on a wheel. Your body is able to reset ever so slightly to a state of homeostasis and relaxation. You are able to gain perspective on your anxieties and understand that you are not forced to be overwhelmed—it was your choice all along.

Again, if it sounds too simplistic, rest assured, studies have confirmed that the practice of meditation does indeed have a real effect. MRI scans were taken of volunteers before and after they participated in an eight-week mindfulness course, the results of which make a strong case for meditation being a useful tool for "strengthening" the areas of the brain that are responsible for executive functions and thus self-discipline—specifically the dorsolateral prefrontal cortex, the anterior cingulate cortex, and the orbitofrontal cortex, which are regions all firmly within our logical brain.

Moreover, meditation was shown to shrink the amygdala, a major part of the emotional limbic brain and also the center of the fight-or-flight instinct. All of this means that those who practice mindfulness are less susceptible to fear, emotional impulses, and stress. Mental energy is often sabotaged by emotional impulses and stress, so keeping these under control is helpful in setting the conditions for willpower.

On top of that, scans showed that the gray matter in the prefrontal cortex had become noticeably denser after meditation. The gray matter growth wasn't isolated to just the prefrontal cortex. The brain structure located behind the frontal lobe—the anterior cingulate cortex—also became denser with meditation practice. This brain area has been associated with functions having to do with self-regulation, such as monitoring attention conflicts and allowing for greater cognitive flexibility. In other words, meditation can both reduce the feelings and emotions that make us lose self-control, and increase our ability to manage those feelings by physically improving the brain structures responsible for them.

If mindfulness isn't already a part of your daily routine, consider adding it in as part of your recharging rituals instead of thirty minutes of television. It's common to hear people say they don't have time for meditation, possibly even seeing this as scheduling a time to be unproductive. But if meditating for a few minutes a day can make you more capable of carrying out your intentions just as you want, the increased energy will more than make up for a few minutes of inactivity. Our mental energy needs to recharge, after all.

Takeaways:

- Even after we take care of our physical selves, we can still feel like a piece of pudding: unable to move on our own free will, and generally without strength of structure. As the energy pyramid demonstrates, physical fitness is a requirement, but not a guarantee of energy. Mental and emotional energy tend to be far more powerful than basic physical energy, and mostly, this works against us. Sure, we have the occasional stories of being insanely motivated and working for twenty hours straight, but more often than not, we are saddled into useless states because of emotional or mental energy depletion.
- First we will discuss emotional energy. This concerns how we feel about ourselves, the world, and our place

within it. It involves our sense of confidence, security, anxiety, and feelings. It is influenced by vampiric people, our own negative beliefs, cognitive distortions, and disempowering narratives. All of this amounts to us spending too much time and energy inside our own heads, rather than directing energy into the external world. And for what? Typically, nothing based in reality, as cognitive distortions demonstrate.

- A few of the most well-known and dangerous cognitive distortions are all-or-nothing thinking, personalizing, overgeneralizing, catastrophizing, and jumping to conclusions. An especially notable cognitive distortion that robs us of resilience is emotional reasoning. This is when reality is defined by the emotions we feel at that very moment. Comparisons are not necessarily a cognitive distortion, but they create the same skewed reality and set of expectations. You should evaluate yourself according to your own baseline,

instead of comparing your worst to other people's best.
- To address distorted beliefs and narratives, a dose of cognitive behavioral therapy is necessary. It is a large upfront energy expenditure, but well worth it in the end. For our purposes, thought diaries going through the ABC process work best. We analyze the activating event (or trigger) of an emotion, the emotional reaction itself, and then connect the two by figuring out the underlying beliefs.
- To be sure, there are many types of people we should avoid to keep our emotional energy protected and intact. They're not necessarily simply dramatic or negative people; they're the ones who prioritize themselves and leave you to clean things up. The best we can do is filter these people out, send positivity into the world, and lower our expectations from others.
- Mental energy is more about an exhausted and overwhelmed mind, and you might be surprised as to how easily our minds become mentally fatigued.

The concept of ego depletion shows that even after just a few decisions or bouts of self-control, our mental energy is spent and we are unable to think analytically and critically. Again, we can't necessarily avoid thinking about in-depth topics in our life, but we can simplify and streamline as much as possible. This includes having default decisions in place wherever possible and protecting our mental bandwidth zealously.

- At the heart of mental energy is a sense of stress on the brain—that's something we can battle by inserting mindfulness meditation into our daily or weekly routines. The idea is to unplug your brain from everything possible and quiet the mental chatter. We are aware of the large drains on our mental energy, but the background static is another element that accumulates quite quickly. Keeping calm through mindfulness meditation will also keep your emotions more even-keeled.

Chapter 4. It's in the Cells

So far, we've considered the question of energy on many levels, both macro and micro. How much total energy we possess is an aggregation of how well we're functioning, behaviorally, emotionally, and physically. We can understand that our bodies are a constellation of interrelated systems. Remember, we can't multiply by zero when it comes to energy, or any of these interrelated systems.

But on the physical front, there is actually a bit more to delve into. Boosting energy at the biological level is much more than simply making sure you're getting good sleep and nutrition, though again, those are the prerequisites to begin with.

The entire body is a complex organism that is entirely made up of and dependent on the flow of energy. We've mentioned the role that good diet plays, and the effects of insulin on blood sugar, but let's look a little closer at the finer details of how your body actually generates energy to live from the food you eat. Though a biology lesson might not seem relevant in understanding how you function at work or the enthusiasm you have for your goals and dreams, when you think about it, every action, every choice, every emotion, every organ in your body relies on fundamental chemical and physiological processes.

And the body is nothing if not a simple collection of different types of cells. Thus, it stands to reason that we must look to our cells for that extra advantage in energy.

This chapter looks at the *cellular* mechanisms behind your body's energy processes, specifically the mitochondria and the role they play in creating the energy you need to survive and thrive. You can optimize health by sleeping better, by taking in the right nutrients and so on. But you can take it a step deeper and use a scientific understanding of your own metabolism to boost your health and energy levels. Everything comes down, in some way, to the mitochondria, so let's take a closer look at how they work, and how you can support them.

The Cellular Powerhouse

You were probably told in high school that the mitochondria are the "powerhouses" of the cell. These little organelles inside every cell in your body are responsible for, broadly speaking, the actual process of converting the food you eat into energy that then powers every active process in the rest of your body. As you sit and read this right now, your mitochondria are working hard to power every twitch of every muscle, your digestion, the heat in your skin, even the electrochemical thoughts zapping around in your brain. Mitochondria themselves are not the most important aspect of this process; rather, it's what they create that matters most: ATP.

ATP, or adenosine triphosphate, is thought of as a molecular "currency" that your body uses to deal in energy. The energy in food is stored in the bonds that hold the atoms of your body's molecules together. When these bonds are broken within the mitochondria, energy is released, captured, and stored for your use. This energy is essentially ATP. ATP is the body's way of capturing and holding this energy to store and use later. Cells in your body that use a lot of energy—like in the heart, muscles, or the brain—consequently contain cells that are packed with mitochondria, and thus ATP.

It's simple: without ATP, there is no energy (i.e. life!), and without mitochondria, there is no ATP. So, if you're really concerned about your well-being and enhancing energy levels, you have to make sure your mitochondrial health is top notch before you do anything else.

A crucial point is that mitochondrial dysfunction is strongly linked with aging. The connection gets overly complex for our purposes, but there are several theories as to why these little cell batteries lose function over time. One is that the very nature of aerobic respiration is damaging to cells, since the process called oxidative phosphorylation within the mitochondrial membranes releases damaging free radicals. Another theory, in keeping with other general theories of ageing, is that repeated cell division allows cell mutations to accumulate with time, eventually inhibiting mitochondrial function. NAD+, an essential coenzyme in the mitochondrial mechanism, is found to decrease aging in some animal studies, but more research is needed to be conclusive.

There's not much you can do about your genetically determined number of mitochondria or the amount of ATP you naturally produce, but it turns out there's plenty you can do to support and encourage these elements in the lifestyle choices you make every day. Learning to turn your mitochondrial function up to the max will mean better cognitive function and focus, stronger muscles and better recovery time, slower aging and plenty of energy for life.

As we get older, mitochondria get old and die off. But it's not this die-off that's a problem per se. Mitochondrial biogenesis, or the birth of new mitochondria, should ordinarily replace lost mitochondria, but this process slows down as we age as well. This means that a great place to focus our efforts is on supporting biogenesis. How on earth do you know if your mitochondria are healthy? Well, a microscopic view of deteriorating mitochondria would show increased mitochondrial death, slower regeneration, and a drop in ATP production. Outwardly, physical signs of aging and chronic disease are the result.

Many of us have been taught that getting tired is just a natural part of aging, and that little children can run around with boundless energy but not older adults. But this doesn't have to be true! Fatigue is not a normal part of growing old, but a sign of impaired function right at the cellular level. Losing energy is not inevitable as we age. In fact, many disorders and diseases that result in extreme fatigue—fibromyalgia, chronic fatigue syndrome and even mold-toxin-caused chronic inflammatory response—all have characteristic mitochondrial impairment. Speak to people with these problems and they'll tell you they feel as though their plugs have been pulled, or that their battery is low—and in a cellular sense, this is exactly what is happening!

Mitochondrial dysfunction can be a problem all on its own, but it's also found in many other chronic diseases, from cancer and autoimmune diseases to Alzheimer's and even, according to some, autism. Plenty of disease processes involve mitochondria in one way or another. Though it might not at first seem relevant to focus on the biology of this one tiny organelle, the more you look at it, the more you see that mitochondrial health is synonymous with overall well-being and energy.

So, what should we be doing to make sure we're giving our mitochondria everything they need to provide us with the energy we want? As it turns out, priming our cells for peak energy is pretty common sense, and you may already be doing all the right things. Firstly, take a closer look at your diet. "Mitochondrial toxins" are, as you may have guessed, refined carbs and excess sugar. This is made worse if you eat a high-carb diet but don't do much to immediately burn up that energy. Besides playing havoc on your energy levels and putting you on a roller coaster of blood sugar highs and lows, a carb-heavy diet could be doing more permanent damage to your cells through the generation of free radicals, and even increase your risk in the longer term of Type 2 diabetes. Italian scientists put rats on a diet that was 30 percent pure sugar, and they found significant damage to the liver mitochondria after only eight weeks. Not only that, the sugar-rich diet also significantly reduced the rats' ability to repair the damage and engage in mitochondria biogenesis.

So to start with, cut back or eliminate sugary drinks, sweets, white bread, cakes, and other refined carbs. There's no need to go on a completely zero carb or keto diet. However, when your body is in a ketogenic state, it produces ketones, which have in some cases been shown to scavenge free radicals and decrease oxidative damage, and help with mitochondrial biogenesis. Again, though, it's not 100 percent clear that free radical damage is as crucial as was once thought, so don't feel the need to eliminate all carbs, especially if you'll be cutting down on valuable fiber, minerals and vitamins in the process.

Choose moderate amounts of good-quality protein sources and then healthy fats like avocado, olive oil, nuts and seeds. Forego sugary fruits for colorful, high-fiber vegetables like leafy greens. These contain plant compounds called *polyphenols* which could also help reduce oxidative stress in the body. For fruits, look for blueberries, cherries, blackberries, and plums—their rich color is a clue to their polyphenol content!

Finally, make sure that you're not overeating. Massive energy dumps like this harm insulin levels, but also wreak havoc on mitochondrial function because the mitochondria won't be able to work that fast, and the excess energy will get stored as body fat, which also tends to create damaging free radicals. As a result, you might guess that caloric restriction has been shown to benefit the mitochondria, both through reducing free radicals, and also through improving mitochondrial efficiency. You can also try intermittent fasting or only eating within a narrow eight-hour period in every twenty-four hours. Otherwise, keep an eye on caloric intake and avoid binges, and you are on the right path.

Another way to support your mitochondrial health is via supplementation. Before you take the leap and buy a supplement, bear in mind that many of the recommended supplements have minimal peer-reviewed evidence to back them up. Nevertheless, you may find that as part of a comprehensive program to boost your energy, supplements do add a little something.

Polyphenol extracts can help the body's own defenses against oxidative stress and free radical damage, and are derived from the same fruits and veggies that should already be in your diet. Pyrroloquinoline quinone, or PQQ, is a popular and effective polyphenol supplement. PQQ isn't that abundant in a natural diet, but is found (happily!) in dark chocolate. Glycerophospholipids, or GPLs, are also currently being researched for their benefits on mitochondrial health. These are fat-containing compounds that are essential for building the membranes of organelles within the cells. Mitochondria, being essentially made of extensively folded inner membranes to increase their surface area, can greatly benefit from GPL.

Clinical trials for these kinds of supplements are still underway, and many use other nutrients like CoQ10, NADH or NAD+, L-carnitine, and alpha-ketoglutaric acid. Results are still not conclusive, but if you're curious, there's plenty of anecdotal evidence that these might help with fatigue and boost overall energy levels.

A third way to boost mitochondrial health and therefore energy levels is, perhaps paradoxically, to exercise. If you're already battling fatigue, it may seem quite a stretch to add vigorous exercise into the mix, in the hope that it might give you energy. But the research is pretty clear: exercise is excellent for your mitochondria. Exercise boosts your mood, keeps your body weight down, improves cardiovascular health and flexibility, *and* boosts energy—particularly as you get older.

Exercise of any kind is going to be beneficial, but several studies show that HIIT, or high-intensity interval training, is especially helpful. A 2017 study published in the journal *Cell Metabolism* shows that HIIT makes the mitochondria more structurally robust, resulting in an almost 50 percent increase in mitochondrial capacity—and even more for people who were older. The logical conclusion is that our mitochondria function just like our muscles; if you want to improve your muscles, you wouldn't let them atrophy. Instead, you would challenge them to encourage growth and strength.

Endurance and aerobic exercise may also encourage mitochondrial biogenesis. This includes things like jogging, hiking, and biking. Weight training, although demanding on mitochondrial function, paradoxically strengthens them, and has also been found to improve overall mitochondrial health. High-intensity interval training in particular has been shown to improve all aerobic respiratory functions as well as tone muscles and enhance cardiovascular health.

Finally, in addition to these diet and lifestyle changes, pay attention to actively protecting your mitochondria from environmental toxins that will accelerate their breakdown. This is a relatively new area of study, but environmental toxins like tobacco smoke, heavy metals, and pollution all show the potential to negatively impact the mitochondria's ability to do its job. Though the evidence is currently modest, we already know that smoking and living in smoggy cities isn't great for health in any case.

Even if you don't smoke, try to avoid being around people who do. Secondhand smoke still has similar effects. Heavy metals have been shown to interfere with the enzymes necessary for oxidative phosphorylation in the mitochondrial membranes, and can be found in well water or sometimes in pesticides used on produce.

To protect yourself, consider a water filter and going organic for at least the "dirty dozen" fruit and vegetables, or those that have the highest exposure to pesticides during growing. These are strawberries, spinach, nectarines, apples, grapes, peaches, pears, tomatoes, celery, potatoes, cherries, and sweet bell peppers. It's more important to eat plenty of fruit and vegetables than it is to eat purely organic, but if you can afford it, start with these twelve and pass on organic produce for things that have a heavy peel or skin, or a short growing season.

Overall, the advice for maintaining healthy mitochondria is, unsurprisingly, not that different from the advice for living well in general. Live a healthy lifestyle with plenty of fresh, healthy food rich in antioxidants from fruits and vegetables. Drink plenty of water, sleep well, exercise often and avoid overeating, smoking, and alcohol. Limit exposure to known environmental toxins and, to round out your plan for better energy levels, possibly add a key supplement to give your body what it needs.

Hot and Cold

For the brave, however, there are also a few more interesting things you could try to raise your mitochondrial output and start feeling super energized. "Cold therapy," although it might not sound like fun for some, has been shown to be a powerful tool for physical and psychological well-being, and a firm favorite in the "biohacking" community for kicking your mitochondrial biogenesis up a notch.

To get a sudden blast of cold throughout your body, you don't need to go skinny-dipping in Siberia. Instead, start small by ending every shower with a quick blast with water as cold as you can get it. Even thirty to ninety seconds will do the trick. If you have a pool, a quick dip in very cold water will greatly increase your mitochondrial health, and this works in two ways: first, it essentially gives your mitochondria a stressor to deal with, just like with exercising, and second, when cells grow cold, they contract, and this closer proximity allows mitochondria to function more quickly and efficiently. There's simply a shorter distance for the energy to travel with contraction.

If you're up for the challenge, a bath filled with ice can create an at-home plunge pool, or you could build your own setup using a little DIY knowledge and some creativity. The idea is to give your body cold therapy regularly, using it just the same as you would a supplement or a daily workout.

The great thing about cold therapy is that it's not just good for you physically, but mentally, too. It takes an iron will and a firm resolve to plunge yourself into discomfort this way. But the corresponding sense of mental toughness you acquire can be enormously satisfying. While your mitochondria get a boost, you're simultaneously strengthening yourself mentally and emotionally, showing yourself that you're strong and that you *can* endure pain and come out the other end, better for the experience. What could make you feel more alive and kicking than diving into an icy glacial pool?

Now, while cold can increase the number of mitochondria, heat can on the other hand increase their efficiency. If steam rooms and heat saunas sound more up your alley, you'll be happy to know that fifteen to thirty minutes of extreme heat has been shown to boost mitochondrial function by up to a third. Specifically, when we are undergoing heat therapy in a sweat lodge or sauna, the energetic needs of our mitochondria go up and they respond by using oxygen in the blood more efficiently. This process is called oxidative phosphorylation (OXPHOS). In one study, repeated exposure to heat stress for six days increased mitochondrial function by 28 percent.

In addition, researchers from Brigham Young University studied twenty adult volunteers who had not participated in regular exercise in the three months prior to the study. The research team applied two hours of shortwave diathermy—a type of heat therapy generated by electrical pulses—to the thigh muscles of one leg of each person every day. The researchers based the six-day trial of heat on the minimum amount of exercise needed to measure changes in muscle, or about two hours each day. The therapy sessions increased the temperature of the heated leg by approximately seven degrees F. Each participant's other leg served as a control, receiving no heat therapy or temperature change. The researchers looked at mitochondria content in the muscles on the first day of therapy and twenty-four hours after the last treatment.

Mitochondrial function increased by an average of 28 percent in the heated legs. The concentration of several mitochondrial proteins also rose in the heated legs, again demonstrating that mitochondria health increases as an adaptation, just like muscular strength.

Heat treatments have a long list of well-researched benefits, including better athletic endurance, increased longevity, and better skin. However, this comes with some caveats—if you're a male attempting to conceive any time soon, it's best to give heat therapy a miss.

The Noble Bean

At the beginning of this book, one of the things that may have come to mind when you thought of energy and how to get it was "coffee." Almost all of us drink it or have in the past. Coffee's reputation for being an all-around energy booster is ubiquitous, and many people reach for it first when their energy is flagging and they need to pep up. Though we've explored the many factors that add to a life that is brimming over with energy, this book would be amiss not to mention the noble bean, and its place in a smart energy-management program.

Sadly, though coffee feels as though it gives you a nice buzz, the truth is that when consumed regularly it can actually damage your energy levels. It's counterintuitive, but coffee doesn't actually give you energy at all. When you feel tired and low energy, the neurotransmitter adenosine (this is an inhibitory neurotransmitter that's related to ATP as discussed above) fits into receptors in the brain, and this triggers feelings of sleepiness. When it's late at night and you're nodding off, it's because your adenosine receptors are full.

The caffeine in coffee can also fit into these receptors, except it has an opposite effect—i.e., making us feel wired up and energized. This is because it blocks the adenosine that would ordinarily plug the receptors, and prevents it from instigating any sleepy feelings. Caffeine essentially shuts off adenosine receptors and their fatiguing effects, overall resulting in a stimulant effect. In the short term, this process works quite well, and there are countless studies to prove that caffeine is excellent at boosting energy and cognitive function.

However, your body is pretty clever, and if you drink caffeine daily, it begins to adapt to the fact. After the coffee wears off, your body might double down and produce more adenosine, almost to balance things out. You're then hit with a massive wall of fatigue that is essentially bigger than the tiredness you originally warded off. If you reach for another cup of coffee, you could end up on a nasty energy merry-go-round, drinking more and more caffeine with seemingly diminishing returns. People who try to quit coffee may discover their energy levels completely crash; convinced that the caffeine was the only thing propping them up, they return to drinking it. However, as you can see, caffeine's power is a bit of an illusion.

What's more, consuming coffee daily can chronically overstimulate your adenosine receptors, causing your body to ramp up production of adenosine *and* receptors. What happens then is that your normal energy baseline drops, and you essentially become dependent on caffeine to attain normal levels of energy. Like a drug addict who develops tolerance, you end up drinking more just to stay in the same place, and find it hard to quit without withdrawal. It's a sorry state of affairs. While you may sincerely believe that your coffee is your energy lifeline, all it's really doing is boosting you back up to what used to be your ordinary energy level, before you started consuming caffeine.

You wake up groggy and unrefreshed, your mood is altered for the worse and there's evidence that coffee has a host of other negative effects on the body, not just on energy levels. That being said, coffee does have some benefits, not to mention it's delicious. Eliminating coffee is a great idea, but you could also choose to drink it for a few days and then take a few days' break. If you're a caffeine junkie, you might need to "detox" for a good few weeks first, just to reset your system. Take heart that although you'll feel like you're dying for a few days, your normal energy levels will return.

If you can manage to give up coffee, it won't be long before you start seeing an improvement. Dropping coffee can improve your sleep and help you feel more balanced and level-headed throughout the day. If you suffer from anxiety or depression, you may find that eliminating coffee cuts down on that on-edge feeling and has your moods feeling more stable. Cutting coffee has also been shown to positively affect PMS and menstrual health, so keep this in mind if you find yourself cycling energy-wise throughout the month.

Since coffee is a diuretic (i.e. it causes you to urinate more), you may find you need a few weeks to find a better water equilibrium in your body. Coffee doesn't dehydrate us directly, but can cause us to pass more water, resulting in dehydration which then leads to feeling sluggish and fatigued. If you're quitting coffee, you may find that replacing it with water or tea helps your transition, and will improve the overall quality of your skin and digestion, too. Finally, if you're used to having sugar in your coffee, cutting this out immediately cuts your caloric intake and will help steady your blood sugar levels in the process. Caffeinated drinks that are also heavy in sugar and fat are sheer destruction for your system, deepening your caffeine crash when it happens. Dropping sugar and cream-laden drinks can have you feeling lighter and more refreshed almost instantly, not to mention the benefit of skipping all those empty calories.

If you're not ready to cut the caffeine cord just yet, that's OK. You can still enjoy moderate caffeine intake without jeopardizing your health too much. Aim for no more than 400 mg of caffeine per day (that's about 2 cups), and avoid adding loads of sugar and cream. Skip coffee altogether in the afternoons and go for tea or water instead. Periodically, wean yourself off and have a few caffeine-free weeks. Try decaf, or else mix half decaf with half fully caffeinated for a compromise.

Finally, there's a more serious reason to moderate your coffee intake: adrenal fatigue. Your adrenal glands are responsible for producing stress hormones. If they're constantly overstimulated, they become exhausted and unable to respond, leading to you feeling completely burnt out. Today, many of us live hyper-stressed, chronically "switched-on" lifestyles. It's like being in "fight or flight" mode, but permanently.

Caffeine is notorious for worsening this phenomenon; your daily cup could be sending constant messages to your adrenals to produce more adrenaline and cortisol. Though excellent in genuine emergencies, routinely flooding your system with these hormones just to meet deadlines and pull all-nighters is no good for your long-term health. Caffeine can "burn out" your adrenal glands and leave you depleted. Furthermore, not only could coffee give you heartburn and intestinal difficulty, it can also interfere with calcium metabolism, wreck blood sugar levels, and interfere with medications. All of this adds up to a perfect storm of exhaustion. If you're someone who has fatigue issues, a particularly stressful lifestyle, an autoimmune or hormonal condition, or a recent illness you're trying to overcome, tread carefully when it comes to coffee. It could be the spark that ignites a whole powder keg of adrenal issues for you.

Takeaways:

- We know that the body is made up of interrelated systems, and we already covered the physical aspect of it. But within the physical aspect, there is also a cellular dimension, as our bodies are composed of different types of cells that determine how much energy we have. Specifically, what's crucial is our mitochondria health. Typically dubbed the powerhouse of the cell, mitochondria create ATP, which we can think of as the fuel for our bodies.
- So the overall play is to increase your mitochondrial health, and also

encourage mitochondrial biogenesis, or the growth of additional mitochondria in cells. There are four primary ways we can do this, and unsurprisingly, they must align with living a healthy and balanced lifestyle in general. (1) diet (polyphenols, fasting, no overeating, ketosis); (2) supplements; (3) exercise (HIIT is most effective); and (4) avoiding environmental toxins.
- Another method of improving mitochondrial health is to manipulate hot and cold. Cold therapy works by helping cells contract, which makes ATP creation more efficient and powerful within the mitochondria. Heat therapy works by forcing adaptation.
- Finally, we come to coffee. Coffee has long been hailed as the king of immediate and temporary energy, but we instinctually suspect that it's not the best solution. This turns out to be true, as coffee royally messes with a few key neurotransmitters, which lead to an ever-worsening cycle of requiring more and more caffeine. Even worse, coffee can cause adrenal fatigue; when you feel

alert and "on," adrenaline flows freely. It's really not meant to flow so constantly, as it prevents us from relaxing, and can easily lead to mental and physical exhaustion.

Chapter 5. Energized Productivity

At this point, you've learned about the origins of energy, and probably why you are fatigued more than you want to be. As you've discovered, you are likely engaging in some degree of self-sabotage.

This final chapter is about some psychological techniques to be productive even when your energy is low or lacking. Sometimes changing the perspective or mindset we have toward our work can make the difference. Indeed, sometimes we can feel drained or energized by the same task just depending on how we frame it.

The Physics of Productivity

Who would have thought that productivity and energy could be viewed through the lens of physics, math, and equations? Bestselling author Stephen Guise found a way to do so using Newton's three laws of motion as an analogy to formulate the Three Laws of Productivity.

By dissecting energy as physics concepts and equations with identifiable elements and interactions, you'll identify the specific things you need to do or to avoid in order to add to your productivity. If you know the variables at work when you lack energy, then you'll be able to single out a particular variable and manipulate it, as you're able to do in a mathematical equation.

The three laws of motion were formulated by physicist Sir Isaac Newton in 1687 to explain how physical objects and systems move and are affected by the forces around them. In other words, he's the guy who claims to have conceived of gravity after getting hit by a falling apple. These laws lay the foundation for understanding how things from the smallest machine parts to the largest spacecraft and planets move. Applied to the science of human cognition and behavior, these laws can also illuminate the mechanisms behind our energy—and how to manipulate those mechanisms to drive productivity.

First law of motion. According to Newton's first law of motion, an object at rest tends to remain at rest and an object in motion continues to be in motion unless an outside force acts upon it.

How this law applies to procrastination is glaringly evident: an object at rest tends to remain at rest, which means a person in a state of rest tends to remain at rest—unless some sort of force moves him or her into action. So if you're currently in a state of inaction with regard to your intended task, you'll tend to stay that way unless you're stimulated into motion. Your tendency to leave that task untouched is thus a fundamental law of the universe.

But remember that Newton's first law of motion works the other way, too: an object in motion continues to be in motion, which means a person in a state of action tends to continue moving as well. So if you're currently working on a task, this law of motion states that you'll most likely keep working on that task. *Our energy flows when it starts to flow.*

The most critical element of becoming energized is to find a way to start. Find a way to get moving. Once you get the ball rolling, it gets infinitely easier to keep going until the task is done.

Now, the next question becomes, how do you get started on a task? Writer James Clear suggests following what's known as the two-minute rule as applied to productivity. The rule states that you need to start your task in less than two minutes from the time you start thinking about it. Think of it as a personal contract you strike with yourself. No matter what, you need to start within the next two minutes. Build some momentum and don't give your energy levels the opportunity to pull you back down.

For example, suppose you're tasked to write a report detailing your department's project updates. To beat the inertia of lazing around the entire morning, commit to just jotting down the project title and objectives or expected output within the next two minutes. You don't need to think about doing the rest of it just yet. You only need to start within the next two minutes. This action will help break the inactivity that's been strapping you down, and once you've started writing things down about your project, you'll find it easier to keep going.

Another benefit of abiding by this rule is you'll also be forced to break the task down into smaller and smaller steps, as giving yourself a two-minute limit for starting requires you to think in terms of more manageable chunks of work you can begin quickly and easily.

Note that the two-minute rule doesn't require you to pledge that you finish your task, or even proceed in an orderly manner. It doesn't need you to mind the quality of your output just yet; you can reserve the critiquing and refining for later. It just needs you to start, to get into motion.

With Newton's first law of motion, you'll find that once you start, you will tend to keep going on your task. Energy begets energy. So rather than wait for an enormous amount of energy before starting, just go ahead and start small. You'll find that your motivation and drive will snowball into ever-larger amounts after you've started.

Second law of motion. Newton's second law of motion explains how a particular force affects the rate at which an object is moving. It is represented by the equation *F=ma*, which states that the sum of forces (*F*) acting on an object is the product of that object's mass (*m*, which refers to how much matter there is in an object) and its acceleration (*a*, which is the rate of change in how fast an object is going).

In other words, the second law of motion dictates how much force is needed in order to accelerate an object of a particular mass in a certain direction. And as illustrated by the equation, the relationship between these three variables—force, mass, and acceleration—is proportional. The greater the mass of an object, the greater the force required to accelerate it. Likewise, the faster you need an object to move over time (i.e., accelerate), the greater the force you'll need to apply.

So if you want to accelerate an object—say, a ball—then the amount of force you exert on that ball, as well as the direction of the force you apply, will both make a difference. If more force is applied for the ball to go left than for it to go right, then you can bet that ball will go left.

Still with me?

Applied to energy, this means you'll need to pay attention not only to the amount of work you're doing (magnitude), but also to where you're applying that work (direction). If you work a lot but don't focus all that work in a single direction, then you'll tend to accomplish less than when you direct the same amount of work to only one direction.

The amount of work you're able to do as a person has its limits, so if you want to get the most out of your effort, you need to start being conscious of where that work goes. As Newton's $F=ma$ equation teaches, where you direct your effort is just as important as how much effort you exert. Temptations, distractions, and lack of task prioritization all serve to scatter your energy and effort in different directions, so avoiding those elements is key to optimizing your productivity. Keep your energy focused.

Say you have a myriad of things to accomplish before the day is up—reply to five client emails, read and critique a lengthy research plan, and write a recommendation letter for a former employee.

Applying Newton's second law, you need to recognize that how fast you'll be able to accomplish a particular task depends largely on your ability to focus the effort you exert on that task and that task only. If you insist on scattering the "force" you exert by frequently switching tabs from email to research to letter-writing all throughout the morning, you'll be less likely to accomplish any one of them before the lunch hour. You may even just be switching back and forth on those tasks as a way to procrastinate on all of them.

To remedy this, apply the principle of Newton's second law: exert your energy/force in a single direction for its maximum acceleration.

Third law of motion. This law of motion states that "For every action, there is an equal and opposite reaction." This means that when Object A applies a force on Object B, Object B simultaneously applies a force of the same amount, but of opposite direction, on Object A. For example, when you swim, you apply force on the water as you push it backward. Simultaneously, the water applies a force on you that's equal in magnitude yet opposite in direction, thus pushing you forward.

Applied to the science of productivity and energy, this law reflects how in your own life, there are productive and unproductive forces at work as well. There is a constant battle, and everyone's level of balance is different. For those who are unproductive, their inefficient forces tend to win more often than not.

Productive forces include positivity, atmosphere, environment, social network, focus, and motivation, while unproductive forces include stress, temptation and distraction, unrealistic work goals, and unhealthy lifestyles (e.g., poor diet or lack of sleep). The interaction and balance between these opposite forces is what creates your typical levels of productivity and energy.

This balance could shift either way—it could lead you to be massively productive or severely drained. For example, it may take you just an hour to finish writing a report when you're feeling well-rested and confident in your abilities, but you may need a week to complete the same task when you're stressed out and insecure.

Basing on the applications of Newton's third law of motion, there are two ways you can go about upping your energy levels. The first is to add more productive forces. This is what Stephen Guise refers to as the "power through it" option, in which you simply find a way to pump yourself up with more energy in an attempt to overpower the unproductive forces inhibiting you from working. This strategy may involve such actions as chugging cup after cup of coffee (although we should know the dangers of this by now) and digesting motivational words through books or inspirational videos.

The "power through it" option could work well, but only for a brief time. The problem with this strategy is that you're only covering up the unproductive forces that are still working to undermine your energy, and this tiring task could easily lead to burnout.

As an alternative, Guise suggests dealing with unproductive forces directly through the second option, which is to subtract, if not totally eliminate, counterproductive forces. This strategy involves such actions as reducing the number of tasks you commit to, learning how to say no, and changing your environment in order to simplify your life.

Compared to the first option, which requires you to add more productive forces, this second option simply needs you to release the reservoir of energy already within you by removing the barriers that obstruct it. As you can imagine, this second option is an easier route to success than having to produce energy by attempting to add more positive forces.

For example, say you need to accomplish a year-end evaluation report for your organization's project sponsor. You're aware that you're the type of worker who needs quiet in order to think and work effectively, but your office cubicle is sandwiched between two chatty colleagues. Instead of simply opting to "power through" the task despite the noisy and distracting environment you're in (i.e., attempting to increase your productive forces), consider relocating to a quieter area or politely asking your colleagues to refrain from disturbing you for the next hour or two (i.e., eliminating unproductive forces).

That way, you'll be more motivated to start and keep working on a task, not necessarily because you've upped your willpower, but because you've simply let the natural energy already within you flow unhindered.

Eliminate the Paradox of Choice

While most people tend to think that having choices is good—and the more choices there are, the better—current research on human behavior actually suggests otherwise. In a phenomenon that psychologist Barry Schwartz calls the paradox of choice, people tend to be worse off when they have more options to choose from as opposed to when they have a single course of action available to them.

For example, suppose your company offers multiple types of research grants you can apply for. Pressured to make the "best" choice among all your options and overwhelmed by the details and comparisons you need to sift through in order to do so, you put the whole research thing on the backburner and leave it untouched for years. With zero additional research studies under your belt, you suffer career stagnation simply because in the face of multiple options, you've been too paralyzed to do anything. You wasted your energy on this nonsense and you're still standing at a crossroads. What a waste.

Learning to deal with the paradox of choice is thus a necessary technique to maximize energy. If you've established a mindset that's able to promptly make sound decisions in the face of multiple options, then you'll less likely waste your energy on things that probably don't matter.

The paradox of choice tends to have a negative impact because once people become overwhelmed with too many options, one of two things tends to happen:

One, after making a choice, you may still constantly think about the other options that you didn't choose. For instance, after buying a painting, you may fixate on imagining how great the other paintings you didn't buy would look in place of the one you bought. So you're never really satisfied with the decisions you make because a part of you remains preoccupied with thoughts of all the other options you missed out on. It is the ultimate case of buyer's remorse.

Two, having too many options can subject you to a very difficult time deciding, such that you become paralyzed from making a decision and from doing anything at all. In philosophy, this is illustrated by the paradox of Buridan's ass (quite literally, donkey). Popularized by philosopher Jean Buridan, this paradox tells of a hungry donkey standing between two identical piles of hay. The donkey always chooses the hay closer to him, but this time both piles are of equal distance away. Unable to choose between the two piles, the donkey starves to death.

Applied to the mechanisms of productivity and energy, the paradox of choice thus ultimately saps your energy, as you delay making a decision under the perception of great responsibility, or you spin your wheels uselessly.

To beat the paradox of choice, the key is to set rules and restraints upon yourself. You'll need to find a way to see things in black and white, because gray areas are fertile grounds that breed overthinking and wasting of energy. That spectrum of color is likely to see you get stuck and agonize over which shade of gray is the best choice until you get tired of the uncertainty, lose motivation, and end up unable to make any choice and act at all. When Buridan's donkey saw shades of gray instead of one defined path to one defined dish of food, he faltered and ultimately starved to death.

To avoid falling into that trap and conserve your energy (remember ego depletion?), use the following strategies.

Focus on one factor and willfully ignore everything else. Every option is sure to offer its own pros and cons, and deciding among numerous options is not merely a matter of tabulating which has the most pros and the least cons. Rather, making a choice depends heavily on what you really care about, which often boils down to only one or two critical factors. So instead of having to deal with countless criteria that can overwhelm you from making a choice, focus only on one or two vital factors and ignore the rest. That way, you have a clearer idea about which option is best for you, and you can select it faster, too.

Suppose you need to buy a new microwave and have multiple models lined up in front of you, each with its own set of features and unique innovations. If you don't know which factors you want to focus on, it's easy to get confused by all the bells and whistles that such a large selection offers.

So to make it easier for you to make a choice that's really suited to your needs, decide beforehand on one or two specific features you want to base your decision on—say, size (i.e., must fit your kitchen space) and sensor cooking. With just these two features in mind, you get to eliminate a lot of other models that don't fit the bill, thus effectively narrowing down your choices to make it simpler to select the right one.

Set a time limit on making a decision. Commit to making a decision within, say, two minutes tops. Whatever decision you arrive at by the end of two minutes, stick with it no matter what. This defeats the paradox of choice by putting a cap on the amount of time you spend agonizing over which decision to make. It saves you from suffering the negative consequences of letting things pass you by and spurs you into the action necessary to realize your goals.

For example, imagine you're in charge of choosing and facilitating the venue for your upcoming gala, but you're torn between Venue A and Venue B. You've put off making reservations for weeks now simply because you can't decide which venue would be the better choice. To save yourself from wasting any more energy, set two minutes for you to come up with a decision and pledge to stick with it.

You may go back and forth between the two venues within those two minutes, but once the time is up, whatever venue you settle on should be the one you go for—say, Venue A. To strengthen this strategy (no backsies!), make sure to call and make reservations for Venue A by the end of the two minutes.

Immediately choose a default option and stick with it if no better alternative comes up. Once you've selected one option as the default, you can set a short amount of time to try to find alternatives and weigh them against your default choice. If none of the alternatives measure up to your default, then you just revert to that initial choice. That way, you're ensured of having already made a decision beforehand, which you can simply follow through with once it's time to act.

The fact that you've identified a default already constitutes a choice in itself, one that you'll most likely be inclined to stick with and follow through on.

For example, again imagine you're in charge of choosing the venue for your upcoming gala, but you're so torn between Venue A and Venue B that you've put off facilitating the task altogether.

To save yourself from wasting further energy, you may set Venue A as your default choice, then allow three days to continue searching for other alternatives or comparing the pros and cons between Venue A and Venue B. If by the end of the third day you find yourself either unconvinced by the other options, or so convinced by all of them you're now confused, then just revert to your default choice of Venue A.

That way, you can start moving on with the rest of your event planning instead of faltering because you can't make a choice.

Finally, strive to satisfice your desires more often than not. The word *satisfice* is a combination of the words *satisfy* and *suffice*. It's a term that Herbert Simon coined in the 1950s, and it represents what we should shoot for rather than something that is guaranteed to optimize and maximize our happiness.

Generally, people can be split into two categories: those who seek to satisfice a decision and those who seek to maximize a decision.

Let's suppose you are shopping for a new bike. The maximizer would devote hours to researching their decision and evaluating as many options as possible. They would want to get the best bike possible for their purposes and leave no stone unturned.

They desire 100 percent satisfaction despite the law of diminishing returns and the Pareto principle, which would warn against such measures.

By contrast, the satisficer is just shooting to be satisfied and is looking for an option that suffices for their purposes. They want something that works well enough to make them satisfied and pleased, but not overjoyed or ecstatic. They aim for *good enough* and stop once they find that.

These are very different scales, and for this reason, studies have shown that satisficers tend to be happier with their decisions, while maximizers tend to keep agonizing and thinking about greener pastures.

Maximization represents a conundrum in our modern age, because while it is more possible now than at any other point in human history to get exactly what you want, there is also the paradox of choice, which makes it impossible to be satisfied. On a practical matter, there are few decisions where we should strive to maximize our value. Therefore, put forth proportional effort and just make a choice already.

Most of the time, you simply want something that is reliable and works. Suppose you are in a grocery store and you are trying to pick out the type of peanut butter you want. What should you shoot for here? Satisficing or maximizing? The same type of thinking should apply to 99 percent of our daily decisions.

Otherwise, we are constantly overwhelmed and waste our mental bandwidth where there are diminishing returns. Whatever net benefit the most optimal type of peanut butter brings to your life is likely not worth the extra effort it took to find it.

Motivation (and Energy) Follows Action

A final mindset to embrace in the battle against draining energy is the way in which true energy and the appetite for productivity appears. Most of the time, whatever the real reason is, we end up telling ourselves that if we aren't in the mood (I don't *feel* like it), then it's not getting done.

Look, it would be five-million times easier to achieve our goals if we all knew how to motivate ourselves 100 percent of the time. It would be like pressing a magical button that jolts us out of bed and into work. Whenever our energy is faltering, we could just press the button again, and we'd be injected with another dose of that good stuff and be correspondingly productive. The closest legal method we have to this is coffee, but even that has waning effects.

It's easier to feel motivated when you like a project or when you're doing something you are genuinely passionate about. But let's be realistic—there are days when just the mere act of leaving your bed is a challenge and a huge accomplishment. For most of us, we don't enjoy what we do for a living enough to feel motivated by it. An artist may be inspired and driven to bring her visions into reality, but for the rest of us? We're really just trying to scrape together enough willpower to get us through our days. This is all to clarify motivation's role in taking action and getting started.

Whatever your goals, motivation plays an important role and can spell the difference between success and failure. It's one of the most important ingredients to influence your drive and ambition, but we're thinking about it *all wrong*.

When we think about motivation, we want something that will light a spark in us and make us jump up from the couch and dive deeply into our tasks. We want *motivation that causes action*. There are a few problems with this, namely the fact that you're probably looking for something that doesn't exist, and that's going to keep you waiting on the sidelines, out of action and out of the race. This type of motivation, if you ever find it, is highly unreliable. If you feel that you need motivation that causes action, you are doing it wrong.

For instance, a writer who feels they are unable to write without some form of motivation or inspiration is going to stare at a blank page for hours. End of story.

The truth is, you should plan for life *without* a motivating kick-start. Seeking that motivation creates a prerequisite and additional barrier to action. Get into the habit of proceeding without it. And surprisingly, this is where you'll find what you were seeking. *Action leads to motivation*, more motivation, and eventually momentum.

The more you work for something, the more meaningful it becomes to you. Your own actions will be your fuel to move forward. After you've taken your first step and have seen progress from your efforts, motivation will come easier and more naturally, as will inspiration and discipline. You'll fall into a groove, and suddenly, you'll be in your work mood/mode. The first step will always be the hardest, but the second step won't be quite as difficult.

For repetition's sake, forget motivation; get started, and you'll *become* motivated.

Taking the first step is tough, but consider that aside from motivation, just getting started gives you many other things.

For instance, confidence also follows action. After all, how do you expect to be confident about something when you haven't even tried? A taste of action tells you that everything will be okay and you have nothing to fear. This is confidence rooted in firsthand experience, which is easier to find as opposed to false confidence from trying to convince yourself before the fact that you can do it.

Public speaking is almost always a scary proposition. Consider how you might try to find confidence that causes action: you would tell yourself it will all be fine, imagine the audience in their underwear, and remind yourself of your hours of rehearsal. Now consider how you might find confidence after getting started—how action can cause confidence. "I did it and it was fine" is an easier argument to make versus "I haven't done it yet, but I think it will be fine."

The most important takeaway here is to not wait until you are 100 percent ready before you take the first step, or believe that motivation before action is a necessary part of your process. It will probably never feel like you're completely ready. But starting down the road will motivate you more than anything else will before the fact, so allow your actions to spur you on and build confidence. Change your expectations regarding motivation, and remove the self-imposed requirements you have for yourself.

As a member of the human race, the tendency for procrastination may be hardwired into your limbic system, but that doesn't mean you should forever be a slave to your own primitive drives and impulses. Building positive mindsets will turn you into an individual in better control of those drives and impulses so you can beat the lure of procrastination.

Takeaways:

- Energy has many, many causes and drainers. This final chapter covers how to be productive even in the face of fatigue.
- The first such tactic is to understand how Newton's three laws of motion can apply to energy. Viewing your energy (or lack thereof) as an equation is helpful because it allows you to think through the variables present in your life and learn how to manipulate them. First, an object at rest tends to stay at rest, while an object in motion tends to stay in motion (the first step is the hardest step). Next, the amount of work produced is a product of the focus and the force that is applied toward it (focus your efforts intentionally). Finally, for every action, there is an equal and opposite reaction (take inventory of the productive and unproductive forces present in your life).
- Another factor in energy is the paradox of choice, wherein choices and options are actually detrimental because they cause indecision and plague us with doubt. They might even cause us to act

like Buridan's donkey and proverbially starve to death between two dishes of food. To combat this tendency, get into the habit of setting a time limit on your decisions, making matters black and white, aiming to become satisficed, and immediately picking a default option.
- Finally, understand that motivation and energy are not things that appear spontaneously. They may never appear...*before* the fact. But after you get started, they will almost always appear. Motivation and energy *follow* action, yet most of us are seeking motivation and energy that *create* action. We are doing it backward and just need to get started to feel better, more often than not.

Summary Guide

Chapter 1. Energy Rules Everything

- It's not that self-discipline, habitualized behaviors, and intentional and analytical thinking are useless endeavors. No, these are some of the best changes you can make to your life. But you won't be able to learn or implement them, or benefit from them in any way, unless you simply possess enough energy to use them.
- Energy is the battery for all of our thoughts and behaviors. Without it, no other tactics, techniques, or tips will matter. This is essentially a real-life application of the concept of multiplying by zero. If your mathematical equation includes a zero, that means the overall

result will be zero. This is another way of saying that energy is often the weakest link in the chain, and it is also the most fragile and elusive. It's important.
- The energy pyramid is a helpful way to think about the role of energy and how to manage it. It has four tiers that depend on each other: physical, emotional, mental, and spiritual. It lays out a blueprint we will follow for the rest of the book. The energy pyramid also dictates that we must rest sufficiently or risk burnout, and at the same time make sure we are challenging ourselves and pushing our limits to increase our energy capacity.

Chapter 2. Physical Energy Vampires

- When we talk about energy, we must start with the physical aspect. Our bodies are our engines, and they must be properly fueled to perform well, or at all. We have to eliminate all of our physical energy vampires and replace them with better habits and awareness. We can take a quick look at what happens when we run out of energy; when we burn out—one of the biggest energy vampires. This is a state of stress and anxiety on the body, where our bodies begin to break down.

- Another prominent energy vampire is a lack of productive and restful sleep. Your sleep hygiene could be terrible and you'd never know it. We should be avoiding blue light before sleeping, lowering stress levels, and keeping a regular sleep schedule. We should also seek to determine our sleep chronotype and understand how it relates to our circadian rhythms. The circadian rhythm directly influences the ultradian rhythm that we abide by when we are awake, and that we take into account with its natural spikes and lulls in energy. Restful sleep is a force multiplier—a quantity that enables great accomplishment in other, unrelated areas.
- Next, we turn to the literal fuel for our bodies, our diets. There is plenty of literature on eating for health, but what

about eating for energy? This concerns something that is lesser known: glycemic index (GI) and glycemic load (GL). We want to ensure that our blood sugar levels are constant and moderate, because if levels are too high or too low, it creates a predictable crash in energy. Thus we must manipulate GI (speed and magnitude of blood sugar from a food) and glycemic load (amount of carbohydrates), as well as timing throughout the day.
- In addition to eating for glucose, we must ensure that we are consuming enough essential vitamins and minerals. We shouldn't be deficient in anything, and we can enhance our energy through specific nootropics, or compounds that give a boost to our physiological states.
- Water is important. Drink more water, hydrate your brain, and keep your energy up.

Chapter 3. Emotional and Mental Energy Vampires

- Even after we take care of our physical selves, we can still feel like a piece of pudding: unable to move on our own free will, and generally without strength of structure. As the energy pyramid demonstrates, physical fitness is a requirement, but not a guarantee of energy. Mental and emotional energy tend to be far more powerful than basic physical energy, and mostly, this works against us. Sure, we have the occasional stories of being insanely motivated and working for twenty hours straight, but more often than not, we are saddled into useless states because of emotional or mental energy depletion.
- First we will discuss emotional energy. This concerns how we feel about ourselves, the world, and our place within it. It involves our sense of confidence, security, anxiety, and feelings. It is influenced by vampiric people, our own negative beliefs, cognitive distortions, and disempowering narratives. All of this amounts to us spending too much time and energy inside our own heads, rather

than directing energy into the external world. And for what? Typically, nothing based in reality, as cognitive distortions demonstrate.

- A few of the most well-known and dangerous cognitive distortions are all-or-nothing thinking, personalizing, overgeneralizing, catastrophizing, and jumping to conclusions. An especially notable cognitive distortion that robs us of resilience is emotional reasoning. This is when reality is defined by the emotions we feel at that very moment. Comparisons are not necessarily a cognitive distortion, but they create the same skewed reality and set of expectations. You should evaluate yourself according to your own baseline, instead of comparing your worst to other people's best.
- To address distorted beliefs and narratives, a dose of cognitive behavioral therapy is necessary. It is a large upfront energy expenditure, but well worth it in the end. For our purposes, thought diaries going through the ABC process work best. We analyze

the activating event (or trigger) of an emotion, the emotional reaction itself, and then connect the two by figuring out the underlying beliefs.
- To be sure, there are many types of people we should avoid to keep our emotional energy protected and intact. They're not necessarily simply dramatic or negative people; they're the ones who prioritize themselves and leave you to clean things up. The best we can do is filter these people out, send positivity into the world, and lower our expectations from others.
- Mental energy is more about an exhausted and overwhelmed mind, and you might be surprised as to how easily our minds become mentally fatigued. The concept of ego depletion shows that even after just a few decisions or bouts of self-control, our mental energy is spent and we are unable to think analytically and critically. Again, we can't necessarily avoid thinking about in-depth topics in our life, but we can simplify and streamline as much as possible. This includes having default

decisions in place wherever possible and protecting our mental bandwidth zealously.
- At the heart of mental energy is a sense of stress on the brain—that's something we can battle by inserting mindfulness meditation into our daily or weekly routines. The idea is to unplug your brain from everything possible and quiet the mental chatter. We are aware of the large drains on our mental energy, but the background static is another element that accumulates quite quickly. Keeping calm through mindfulness meditation will also keep your emotions more even-keeled.

Chapter 4. It's in the Cells

- We know that the body is made up of interrelated systems, and we already covered the physical aspect of it. But within the physical aspect, there is also a cellular dimension, as our bodies are composed of different types of cells that determine how much energy we have. Specifically, what's crucial is our mitochondria health. Typically dubbed the powerhouse of the cell, mitochondria create ATP, which we can think of as the fuel for our bodies.

- So the overall play is to increase your mitochondrial health, and also encourage mitochondrial biogenesis, or the growth of additional mitochondria in cells. There are four primary ways we can do this, and unsurprisingly, they must align with living a healthy and balanced lifestyle in general. (1) diet (polyphenols, fasting, no overeating, ketosis); (2) supplements; (3) exercise (HIIT is most effective); and (4) avoiding environmental toxins.
- Another method of improving mitochondrial health is to manipulate hot and cold. Cold therapy works by helping cells contract, which makes ATP creation more efficient and powerful within the mitochondria. Heat therapy works by forcing adaptation.
- Finally, we come to coffee. Coffee has long been hailed as the king of immediate and temporary energy, but we instinctually suspect that it's not the

best solution. This turns out to be true, as coffee royally messes with a few key neurotransmitters, which lead to an ever-worsening cycle of requiring more and more caffeine. Even worse, coffee can cause adrenal fatigue; when you feel alert and "on," adrenaline flows freely. It's really not meant to flow so constantly, as it prevents us from relaxing, and can easily lead to mental and physical exhaustion.

Chapter 5. Energized Productivity

- Energy has many, many causes and drainers. This final chapter covers how to be productive even in the face of fatigue.
- The first such tactic is to understand how Newton's three laws of motion can apply to energy. Viewing your energy (or lack thereof) as an equation is helpful because it allows you to think through the variables present in your life and learn how to manipulate them. First, an object at rest tends to stay at rest, while an object in motion tends to

stay in motion (the first step is the hardest step). Next, the amount of work produced is a product of the focus and the force that is applied toward it (focus your efforts intentionally). Finally, for every action, there is an equal and opposite reaction (take inventory of the productive and unproductive forces present in your life).
- Another factor in energy is the paradox of choice, wherein choices and options are actually detrimental because they cause indecision and plague us with doubt. They might even cause us to act like Buridan's donkey and proverbially starve to death between two dishes of food. To combat this tendency, get into the habit of setting a time limit on your decisions, making matters black and white, aiming to become satisficed, and immediately picking a default option.
- Finally, understand that motivation and energy are not things that appear spontaneously. They may never appear...*before* the fact. But after you get started, they will almost always appear. Motivation and energy *follow* action, yet

most of us are seeking motivation and energy that *create* action. We are doing it backward and just need to get started to feel better, more often than not.

CPSIA information can be obtained
at www.ICGtesting.com
Printed in the USA
BVHW062136041022
648622BV00003B/347

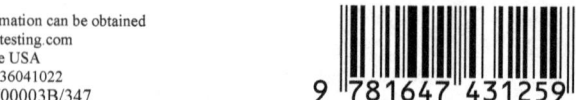